D

J D Stockholm

J D STOCKHOLM

## *What readers are saying:*

*"Fresh writing style."*

*"… a sobering look into the terrifying world of child abuse as seen through the survivor's eyes… a five-year-old boy."*

*"The reader is easily transported."*

*"I found myself praying for him throughout the book. I found myself cursing and talking out loud and comforting him."*

*"… then there was his childlike vocabulary, his bright mind, his utterly sweet spirit, even his ignorance of what was actually happening on every level, it was all like a buffer against the horror of it."*

ISBN-13:978-1478197591

ISBN-10:1478197595

Copyright © 2012 J D Stockholm

All Rights Reserved

# DEAR TEDDY

To Jamie.

I wrote this story for you. The story of a little boy a long time ago. I never realised how big his voice really was, or even what he meant to me. Maybe I don't always say it. Maybe I don't always feel it. . I'm glad that you are part of my life. Without your strength and courage, perhaps this story would not be possible. I owe the words to you.

Thank you.

\*\*\*

Thank you to Diane for all your support, smacks, jabs, pokes and generally being there through all the hard times that came about while I wrote this. Thank you to Sue for taking the time to read through this to make sure that it was right. Thank you to Mr. Ted. For always holding my hand when I needed it and for still watching over me.

Based on a true story. Though names, places and dates may have been changed.

Contact

dearmrted@gmail.com

http://jdstockholm.com/

http://www.facebook.com/dearmrted

# J D STOCKHOLM

## His Name Is Ted.

His name is ted

But he doesn't understand

I lay there waiting

Holding his hand

Night has come

And I lie and stare

I cannot close my eyes

I do not dare

I clutch his paw

And hold on tight

Maybe my prayers

will be answered tonight

# DEAR TEDDY

The floor boards creak

outside my door

And I know I have been bad

Once more


The tears fall

Before he starts

Another night

And a broken heart


He takes my clothes

And my soul

I cannot get back

The innocence he stole


I cry for my mum

## J D STOCKHOLM

But she does not come

No chance of rescue

For her evil son


My teddy bear

Held tight in bed

He will never tell

The secrets I said.

# DEAR TEDDY

## ONE

Little boy, little boy,
Curled in a ball.
I know your secrets,
I know them all.

    Don't tell. Don't tell. It's a secret, you know.

    It was special, my Nan said, "Don't tell your mother," so I promised I wouldn't. I had to tell Mr. Ted, of course. I told him. He knew everything. He looked after me. He was magic and he kept them away; the bad people that came.

    We were going to the circus. I had never seen one before, not in real life, just on the television or in books at school. I asked Mr. Ted what he thought about them, but he didn't know. He had never been either.

    He wasn't allowed to come with us. "He'll get lost if you take him," my Nan said. "And then what will you tell your mother?"

    I thought about that; Mr. Ted all alone in

the dark or that maybe someone else would find him and take him home. What would I do then? He wouldn't be able to find his way home and then the bad man would get me.

I knew my Nan was right, but it still made me sad. I didn't want to leave him home alone. I did as I was told. I took him to my room and placed him in the bed; just his head and his arms popping out from under the covers.

"I'll tell you all about it," I said to him before I left. "I promise."

The circus was big. Bigger than anything I had ever seen before. I wished I could tell my mum and dad about it, but my Nan said they wouldn't understand and so I promised not to tell. But I could tell Mr. Ted. He wouldn't tell anyone.

There were clowns with big feet and funny coloured hair. People on ropes that swung through the air. I wondered how they didn't fall. It was like flying. Everyone cheered when the man caught the girl and I jumped up. I was afraid he would miss. I had forgotten myself and I winced with the pain.

# DEAR TEDDY

My Nan didn't see. I didn't want her to know. She would ask me questions and want to look, but then she would know I had been bad.

At the end of the show when it went dark, I sat and waited. I didn't want it to be over. No one else moved either. They waited just like I did and when the small lights lit the ground, like tiny stars down below; I couldn't wait as I leaned forward.

Four platforms raised and out came elephants and dancers. They stood in the corners. A man came out; my Nan said he was called the ringmaster. He wore a long coat. It was red and black, and his hat was tall like the ones that were in my books. He was real.

Music began and the crowd started to clap. It was so loud I could feel it in my chest like a heartbeat.

Happy Birthday he sang and listed some names. He said my name and two other boys. I gasped and stared as my Nan leaned over my shoulder and smiled.

"That's me?" I asked her and she nodded

with a grin.

"Go on," she said, as the ringmaster called us down to come and stand with him. He made everyone sing to us like we were something special. My Nan took a picture.

When it was over and we went home again, I got Mr. Ted and we sat in our spot by the fire between the hearth and the chair; out of the way. I had a certificate; it said Happy Birthday and my name in big red letters.

I told Mr. Ted about the way the clowns made each other fall over. I told him about the animals and the flying people. I told him about what my Nan had said and the song that was sung. She told me I was five and it was my birthday. I had never had a birthday before. My brother had them. He'd had three, but my mum told me that children from the devil didn't have birthdays.

That's where I was from. My mum told me that my dad had forced her and babies made that way came from Satan. But it was okay. She was going to cure me and I wouldn't be evil anymore and then she could love me. I couldn't wait. I didn't need birthdays.

When she gave me Mr. Ted, she told me he was a gift. I had to keep him safe and look after him, and at night when I was sleeping and the evil came into the house, it wouldn't be able to take me because he was there and he wouldn't let them.

He had some fur missing and the squeak in his tummy didn't work anymore, but I didn't mind. He was mine and he listened. He was my friend.

I sat Mr. Ted on my knee and put my certificate into my scrapbook. I stayed quiet by the fire and waited for my mum and dad to come home. I didn't know where they had gone, but when they came back; my dad threw a black sack at me.

"We got you some new clothes," he said. "You better look after them or there won't be anymore."

I nodded at him, pulled the bag close and said thank you, but I didn't open the bag. I had done that once before and my mum got mad. She said that because I was the devil's child, I was greedy, so I just stayed where I was. I smiled at my mum and dad and hoped that they see I liked what they had bought for me.

My Nan could go because my parents were home. She put on her coat and smiled down at me. I was sad because she was leaving. I didn't want her to go, but I didn't say anything. I didn't move as she went to leave. I knew if I did, I would be in trouble, so instead, I listened and said thank you to her in my mind for my day. And then she was gone and I was alone.

Mr Ted.

I got to go to the circus today. It is my birthday. I am five years old. I wish I got to take you too. Maybe we can draw a circus and you can see what it is like. It's a secret. You can't tell my Mummy. She will shout at my Nan.

## DEAR TEDDY

## TWO

Little boy, little boy,
Bow your head,
Don't listen to his words,
Ignore what he said.

No food for me. No seat. No plate. It was spaghetti hoops with toast and boiled eggs. My brother ate and I just watched. I could feel the food in my mouth. Like pretend. I bet it tasted good.

My dad was mad. "Ungrateful kids don't get to eat," he said. "If you can't appreciate when we buy you things then why should we give you food that I worked for? It's all take with you."

I didn't know how to appreciate things. I didn't know what it was. I sat Mr. Ted on my knee and I opened the black sack. Maybe I could ask Mr. Ted later what appreciate was.

There were new clothes inside. Just for me. The ones I had were all too small or I made them ripped. I wondered if the boy that owned these clothes first, missed them. I knew when my mum and dad took my things when I wasn't home. It made me sad. I wondered if this boy was sad about his clothes. I was sorry for taking his things.

I took out the first thing and looked at my dad. I didn't know what was right. I only ever had bad thoughts.

"I like it," I said.

My dad took a drink from his can. "You like it? That's all you can say?"

I nodded. I nodded so hard it shook my head nearly off and made me dizzy.

"Well that's just great," he said. "I should just give them to your brother, he'd be grateful for them. I should have known better. Next time I'll leave you in those rags so the kids at school can keep on at you."

"I do want them. I do," I said. Bad boy. Bad boy. Always.

I wanted Mr. Ted to tell me what to do; to tell me the answer. I hugged him to me. My tummy hurt and my hands were shaking. I kept being bad and I couldn't make it stop. I was evil inside like my mum said.

# DEAR TEDDY

I took more things from the bag. I looked at them and folded them. I folded them good like my mum wanted. My dad was watching. I looked faster. My fastest.

My dad came over and I put my head down, bowed it like Mr. Ted told me to do. I didn't close my eyes. Didn't blink. No crying allowed. How dare I cry for the bad things I did.

Please tell my dad I'm sorry. Please tell the bad man it was on accident. I closed my eyes and hugged myself. The bad man could read my mind. He knew what I thought. He punished me for my badness.

I wanted to go to sleep and hide.

My dad hit me across my head. I tried not to move. I just cried. I tried not to, but I couldn't help it. My eyes wanted to cry. He was angry with me for the way I was bad. I wished he knew I was sorry.
He put his hand in my hair. Pulled my head back. Stared me in the face. "Get this crap away and then get ready for bed," he said.

My heart started to shake. My mouth didn't stop shivering as I looked at the door and thought about the stairs. Would he be waiting? The man? Maybe if I hurt me first he wouldn't do it. I could tell him I knew I was bad. I was learning. I could be mad at myself for being so bad.

I reached into my jumper and pinched at my skin. Harder and harder. Please don't come in. I did it for you. I did it so hard that I hoped he would know. Maybe Mr. Ted could tell him. He could tell the bad man that it was done already.

Because I was slow to get up, my dad pulled my arm. He yanked me to my feet and I nearly dropped Mr. Ted. "Get upstairs," he shouted. He dragged me to the door and pushed me out of the room.

I went to the bedroom and got my pyjamas from the box near the window. I stared at the door. I had to watch in case he came. He liked to sneak up on me. It made me scared.

I got changed and waited. I didn't have a bed. My mum said they didn't have the money to buy one. I slept on the box or sometimes in the bed if I'd been good and then my dad would let me sleep with them. I wondered if Jack Frost would come through the window at night and make me frozen.

I liked Jack Frost. He made the ground sparkle. Like where Superman lived. If I could be liked Superman maybe my mum and dad would like me. Maybe I would be good and not make everyone mad all the time.

When I was dressed I stood still. He hadn't said to get in bed so I didn't. I stayed still. As still as a statue. Not moving. I held my breath to keep me all still. If I kept my face to the door and just moved my eyes then the bad man wouldn't know I wasn't looking. He would see my face pointing the right way and wouldn't come in.

I heard footsteps.

One.

Two.

Three. Four. Five. Once I caught a fish alive

They were slow. Not shuffled. They were my mums. I knew her walk. I told Mr. Ted so he knew too. When I was asleep he could wake me if he heard the bad man coming.

She came into the room but she didn't talk to me. She had my medicine to make me better so I didn't be evil. I didn't like the medicine. It tasted funny. Not like the ones from the doctors. They tasted like banana or strawberry. I liked the strawberry the best. I had never had a real strawberry. I wanted to though because I liked the doctor's medicine.

She let me get in bed. I put Mr. Ted by the edge. We had a deal to do it that way. When the bad man came he would get Mr. Ted first and I would have time to get away.

I listened as my mum went downstairs and when she came back up later to put my brother to bed. I pretended to be asleep. I closed my eyes. My brother had a room. It was little and next to my mum and dad's. He had Donald Duck painted on the door. My dad had done it. He had so many toys. He was very lucky. Maybe one day I'd be as good as him and I could have a room with a bed and toys from the shops, and a magic light that put a train on the wall.

My eyes were sleepy. I wasn't. They kept closing. I tried to make them stay open. I kept very still so the bad man wouldn't know I was in the room. If I didn't move he wouldn't know I was there.

I went to sleep.

The bang. It was Mr. Ted telling me to wake up.

He was here.

He was here.

I screamed for my mum. Screamed her name. So loud. As loud as I could. Deep breath and a shout. She didn't hear me. The bad man pulled at my covers and I held on tight. He pulled hard and I screamed. No one came. No one heard me. I cried. The bad man had made them all go to sleep.

He pulled off my covers. He got me. His hand on my leg as he pulled at my clothes.

Darkness.

Mr Ted.

Please tell the bad man I'm sorry. I didn't mean to be bad. He got me again. I promise to be good next time. Please tell him that I liked my clothes that my Daddy got me. I won't be bad ever again.

## THREE

Little boy, little boy,
Yell for your mum,
The bad man is gone,
He's finished, he's done.

It was dark. I was afraid. Scaredy cat. The covers were all around me. Tucked in so tight.

Don't make a sound. Don't breath. Don't move.

I didn't know where Mr. Ted was. I hoped he was okay. I hoped he wasn't torn into a million pieces. Not like my things. Not like how my Dad did to my pictures when he got mad. Not Mr. Ted.  Please be okay.

There was no one there. No bad man. He'd gone. Gone when I was sleeping.

I hoped.

I listened. I couldn't hear him breathing. Like a monster in the dark. Like the ones that hid under beds.

Maybe he was tricking me.

I tried to move. The covers were tucked down tight. They were tucked in like my mum used to do to my brother. It was to keep him safe she said.

He stayed safe from the bad man.

The bad man is good at hide and seek. Better than me. I always get found.

Tag you're it. Always me. Stupid boy.

Deep breath. Deep breath. One, two, three. I yelled for my mum. Screamed loud enough to wake the dead my mum said. I didn't want to wake the dead.

Maybe if I waked my Gaga, then my Nan didn't be sad anymore. I could share cornflakes with him again from his pan. It was a secret. I didn't tell my mum. I kept that secret. I was a good secret keeper. My mum didn't know about the cornflakes. She would have been mad.

He shared with me so I would grow to be big and strong. "Big enough to climb Mount Everest," he said.

I didn't know what a Mount Everest was. I asked Mr. Ted, but he didn't know. We couldn't even find one in our picture books.

Maybe it was bigger than a beanstalk. I had seen those. There is a giant that lives at the top and he tries to eat you. He tried to eat a boy named Jack once. I didn't want to see no giants.

But maybe I could raise the dead and see my Gaga. I could eat cornflakes and climb Mount Everest.

I just had to learn to be a good boy first.

My mum came this time. She had woken from the bad man's spell. She ran up the stairs. I knew it was her. I heard her feet. When I called again she answered me and told me she was coming.

"What have you done?" she asked.

I didn't tell her because it was the bad man. If I talked about the bad man he would be mad and then he would get me. He wouldn't ever stop. He would make sure I didn't see my family again.

I told my mum once. She said that the bad man was a demon. She said that because I was evil he comes into the house. She said when I get better he will go away. She told me not to tell anyone because they didn't understand demons.

# DEAR TEDDY

Cross my heart and hope to die. I won't tell anyone. The bad man would get mad if I did.

He didn't like me telling Mr. Ted. But Mr. Ted was good at keeping secrets. He never tells. He is my friend.

My mum untucked me from the bed. The covers were tucked in everywhere. Even around my head. I don't know why the bad man did that. It made it hard to breathe. She told me to get off the bed. I did. She pulled my pants down and told me to get out of them. I did that too.

There was blood in my clothes. I hoped that she didn't see. If she saw she would laugh at me and then I would be bad again. The bad man would come because I got to be naughty. My mum said that only girls did that in their clothes.

My dad always said that I am a big girl's blouse. I can't tell them I'm not a girl. Because the bad man did it while I was sleeping. He put it there.

I had scratches all down my arms and legs too. There are some on my back. He liked to scratch me. It made my clothes hurt. My mum said I did it to myself.

She told people that there is something wrong with me that way.

I'm never going to be like Superman. He's good all the time and I am bad.

My mum sent me to the bathroom. "Make sure you wash properly," she said. "I don't want to have to explain to your father why you're not clean."

I got the cloth from the side of the bath and filled the sink. Sometimes I rub so hard that it made my skin red and sore. I didn't know why I did that. I just wanted to be clean enough. Maybe I am strange like my mum said.

My dad always said that people that are strange get sent to prison. He said it's a special prison with mad people. People that don't know things. I didn't want to be locked in with them. But I had to wash my skin until it hurt. If I didn't I felt bad.

When I went back to the bedroom my mum told me to lie down on the floor. She used powder and cream like Janet her bestest friend did on baby Amy. I'm wasn't allowed near Amy. Like I didn't get to be allowed near my brother. Not until I got better. I didn't want to make them evil.

Amy had a nappy. That was why she had powder and cream. It was funny when her mummy put it on. The powder got up into the air like a cloud. It maked my throat feel funny. I didn't wear nappies. I got to be a big boy. I didn't need them.

I didn't like the cream. It maked me feel funny and my mum's nails hurt. She scratched me by accident sometimes. I just wanted to go to sleep. I knew the bad man didn't get to come now because my mum always climbed in bed next to me. I didn't know where my dad was. Maybe he was out on his bike with his friends.

When I get big and strong I will be like my dad and have a bike.

Mr Ted.

My tummy hurts. The bad man made lots of scratches. My mum said he didn't be real. My Mum got me out of the bed. She said I got myself all covered up.

But it was the bad man. But you can't tell anyone. He might get mad.

# DEAR TEDDY

## FOUR

Little boy, little boy.
Swallow the cure,
She'll make you better,
Not evil, but pure.

    I liked when my mum came upstairs at night. She made it feel safe up there for me. She always smelt of perfume. She got undressed into her nightwear and climbed into her side of the bed. If had been a good boy or if my dad wasn't home, I got allowed to sleep on his side.

    Even Mr. Ted could sleep in bed with me. I kept him by the edge. My mum didn't mind. He slept there just in case the bad man came back.

    I didn't mind sleeping on the box. It had a purple lid on it. It was soft and if I curled up I could fit. Just right.

    But, I didn't like sleeping on the box when it was cold. If I had been bad it was worse because there was no blanket. I didn't deserve them my dad said. I didn't like it when I was cold. Mr. Ted would sleep just in front of my face. When I breathed, it made my face warm. Sometimes, I would put my hands there too so they could get warm.

I didn't like it when my hands were cold. It made them hurt. I didn't like lying on the box with no covers when I got sick. I was sick a lot and it made me cold inside my arms and legs. My mum said it was just the cure working and if I wanted to be a good boy then I had to suffer some. "We all make sacrifices," she said.

I didn't like when it made me sick from my tummy. If I didn't make it to the bowl in time my mum would get mad at me. Sometimes, if my dad was home he would give me a clip around the ear. If I cleaned it up myself it didn't make him so mad.

I was awake before my mum. When that happened, she said I could go downstairs and put the television on as long as I was quiet. I did go down, but I didn't put the television on. It got me into trouble.

My dad was home when I got up. I hadn't heard him come in and I didn't talk to him. He slept in the chair by the fire. I sat down on the floor and waited for him to wake. Mr. Ted and I wrote stories.

When my dad did wake and got ready for work, I didn't move. Sometimes he was too tired and it made him mad at me. He worked fixing bikes and cars. He had a motorbike. I was never allowed on it. Or to touch it. Sometimes, when I was really bad, I wasn't allowed to look at it.

That morning he wasn't mad. He made me breakfast. He did that sometimes. Usually porridge. Then he would sit at the table and smoke. Sometimes, he would ask me what I had been doing at school.

I didn't always get breakfast. Maybe, I was just too bad to get food, but we didn't have a lot of money. My dad said that my mum spent it all on smoking. My mum said my dad spent it on his cheap trollops.

I didn't know what a trollop was, but he picked them up at a school. Sometimes, they would fight about it. She would hit him until he had to hit her back. I didn't like when they had fights. I was afraid they would hurt each other.

When I had been good and we had milk and I got breakfast I ate it as slow as I could. I tried to be quiet so my mum didn't see me. She gave me my medicine when I was finished eating. If I was too slow, she got to take the food away.

I knew I had to take the medicine. Sometimes, it made me lots of sick that I couldn't breathe. My mum got mad when that happened. She said I was keeping the evil inside. She told me that it was on purpose. That the devil told me to be bad. When that happened I had to have my night time medicine and then the bad man came.

When my mum came down I hadn't finished my porridge. She got mad at me. I didn't know what I had done. I had stayed quiet. She hadn't spoken to my dad. Maybe they were both mad at me.

When my dad went to work my mum sat my brother in his chair next to me. I wasn't allowed to touch him. She made me move to the wall so he didn't get evil too. "Eat your damn cereal and come into the kitchen when you're done," she said to me. She gave my brother his breakfast.

My food was hard to eat. I wished Mr. Ted ate real food and not like pretend. Then he could help me eat it. It made me feel sick trying to swallow.

Maybe I had taken too long to eat. Or it was because I had been bad. My mum came into the room and sat down next to me. She stared at me. I tried not to look at her. It made it hard for me to eat. I didn't know what I had done, but I was sorry.

"Eat faster," she said.

I tried. I promised I was trying. I put the food in my mouth, but it didn't swallow. She got mad at me. She took the spoon from my hand. When I said I was sorry, she took Mr. Ted and gave him to my brother.

I tried not to cry. I tried really hard. It was bad if I cried, but my eyes didn't stop it. She took the spoon and got my breakfast. She filled the spoon all the way up.

"Open your mouth," she said.

I didn't want to. I didn't like how it felt. "It's lumpy," I said.

"Open your mouth," she said again. She put her hands on my nose. The spoon hurt my gums. My brother started to cry and my mum got mad at me for it.

"Look what you did," she said. She took my breakfast away and told me to get in the kitchen.

I was sorry.

Mr Ted.

Tell my Mummy I'm sorry. I'm sorry I'm so bad all the time. Tell her I got scared of the medicine. It tasted yucky. I didn't mean to be bad. I'm just bad inside. From the devil and my evilness. Please make her believe me. I'm sorry.

# DEAR TEDDY

## FIVE

Little boy, little boy.
Dry those tears,
She doesn't care,
For your scares or fears.

I knew I wasn't allowed to sit. Not until I got told. Good boys do as they are told. "If you want to be good, you better do as I damn well say. No moving, no fidgeting. You'll be lucky if I let you breathe," she said.

So I knew. I did as I was told like a good boy. Doing as she damn well said.

My mum made my medicine. She made it in my cow cup while I stood and did as I was told. No fidgeting. No moving. Still like a statue.

My cow cup wasn't a cow cup anymore. The picture all cleaned off. But I knew it had been a cow. It was still my cow cup. My Nan gave it to me. I always used it when she shared hot tea. I liked my Nans tea. It was sweet and made me warm inside. We didn't tell my mum about the tea. She would get mad. The tea stopped me being cold.

Sometimes I kept my toys in my cow cup. Larry the Lamb. He was made of Lego. His legs squeaked when he sat. My toy car too. It was small and green. The glass was gone. But it was the fastest car in the world. Larry wasn't good at driving it. He always fell off when it got too fast. I made him stick with some sticky ball my Nan gave me. He wasn't good at balancing.

I was. I could stand on one foot for a long time. My Mum had made me do it one day. I was glad I was so good. She said I had to stand on one foot because the other had dog muck on the bottom. She said I had to think about where I was going in future. I didn't know where I was going so I didn't know what I was supposed to think about. But I did stand on one leg like she said. For a long time until my leg got tired.

I stood in the kitchen waiting like she said. On two legs. As my mum mixed my medicine in my cup. So still. Quiet as a mouse. I didn't make a noise. My brother sat on the floor. He had a biscuit. He always got one after breakfast. Because he was a good boy. I wished I could have one too, but they were his. I wasn't good enough for biscuits.

My mum was mad at me. Her eyes looked like fire. I didn't like it when she looked like that. I told her I was sorry. I didn't know what I was sorry for. Maybe I had been bad and not known about it. I was always bad. Sometimes it happened on accident.

"Open your mouth," she said and I did.

The spoon was big and cold. It bashed my tooth and I jumped. She made my tooth jump. She pushed the spoon all the way in my mouth. I thought she was going to make me swallow it too. It went in deep and made my neck do a funny hiccup. It maked my tummy feel funny. Like it got made to jump too.

The medicine was hot. It tasted like fire. My mouth was full. Like sand. Horrible sand like with water. When the sea comes in and makes the castle mushy. I wondered if my mum has given me sand. I didn't remember her going to the beach.

I couldn't swallow it. It tasted too bad. I didn't like it. My face scrunched up on its own. My neck wanted to do the hiccup thing. My eyes started to cry and they wouldn't stop. It was sticky in my mouth and I didn't like it.

"Swallow," she said to me.

I did try. My neck wasn't working. I couldn't make it swallow like she said. It tried to turn upside down.

She put her hand over my nose and mouth. I couldn't breathe. I tried, but she held too much. Her hand smelt funny. I couldn't make my mouth swallow. It hurt. I tried. I tried to make it. It made me cough and I pulled her hand. She slapped my leg. I had no pants on. I didn't wear pants in the house. Just a t-shirt and my underwear.

I tried to cry because my leg hurted. I tried to breathe. It worked. I got it to swallow. But I coughed too hard. I couldn't make the cough stop and it made the medicine come back. It scratched inside. It made my tummy hurt. I got sick in my tummy. I couldn't help it. My sick came out and landed on my feet. My mum got mad because it got on the floor too.

She dragged me to the bin. The sick wouldn't stop. It kept coming out on her floor. It maked a line and I didn't get any in the bin.

"Look at the damn mess now," she said. "As if I don't have enough to do in this house."

I tried to tell her I was sorry. I wanted her to know I didn't mean it. It was on accident. She smacked my leg again and then again. She hitted it too hard and I cried too loud. My crying made my brother jump and then he cried too.

She swung me round with my arm. She pulled my underwear down and smacked me lots of times. I don't know how many. The smacking made my tummy hurt again. I tried to tell her I was sorry.

When she let go of me I tried to hug her. I wanted it to not be bad. I wanted her to hug me like she did my brother. Her face was angry again. She bent down. I thought she was going to hug me and I put my arms up.

She hit my hands. Told me to go away. It made my tummy sad and I hugged myself as tight as I could.

I did that sometimes at night. I hug Mr. Ted and me. That's how Mr. Ted hugs me.

"Why would I want to touch you?" she said. "I'm not your friend."

I cried hard and told her I was sorry. I cried so hard to make it better. I told her I was sorry. No one is ever my friend. I am always bad. All the time. I wished she knew I was sorry. I wanted her to be my friend. I wanted to be a good boy, but the evilness gets me.

I tried to clean up. I wanted to help so she didn't get angry. I wanted her to be my friend again.

"Leave it," she yelled at me.

I told her I was sorry. My tummy got sick again. My mum saw what was going to happen. She got my neck and pushed me to the bin. I couldn't be sick on the floor. She pushed my head into the bin so I could be sick in there. I didn't want to make her more busy.

My mum was mad at me again. She dragged me from the kitchen to the back room.

"Don't you dare vomit again," she said. "I've got enough to do without you making more mess."

I nodded and I cried.

She told me to stop crying or she would give me something to cry about. When she went back into the kitchen I had to take my evil away. I wrapped my arms around my legs. My eyes kept crying. They wouldn't stop. My head was sore. I wondered if my head would pop.

Maybe the bad man would come. Maybe he would come in the daytime. When I was really bad he would come in the light time. He hurts me. I didn't want him to hurt me. I didn't want the bad man to come. I wanted my mum to be my friend.

My car had scratchy bits. I hugged Mr. Ted and told him. I wanted him to tell the bad man I took my badness away. I made the car rub my leg. I rubbed it up and down with the scratchy part so Mr. Ted could tell the bad man I got hurted already and he didn't have to do it.

I told Mr. Ted to tell the bad man I made it better. I scratched the car up and down. I did it lots of times. I made it hurt so I cried. If I cried then it would be enough. Mr. Ted would tell the bad man and the bad man would tell my mum I had tried to be good. Maybe he didn't hurt me.

    I told Mr. Ted I am sorry.

Mr Ted.

    I didn't mean to get sick on my Mummy's floor. It was on accident. Please tell the bad man I didn't be bad on purpose. Tell the bad man I make myself cry and he doesn't have to.

# DEAR TEDDY

## SIX

*Little boy, little boy,*
*It's not like pretend,*
*Stay with me, I'm here,*
*Hold my paw till the end.*

My mum didn't talk to me all day. Not one word. Except when she wanted me to move. "Shift," she said, and I did right away. No please and thank you.
I had to say please and thank you. But she didn't. Not when she was talking to a bad boy that was in the way.

I told Mr. Ted how bad I had been. I told him about getting sick on the floor. About how my mum had to clean it, but she was very busy. Maybe there was a magic way to clean it. Getting sick on the floor was bad. It wasn't even cleaning day.

I knew when my dad was home. I knew my mum was telling him what I had done. She shouted loud. My brother sat on the floor. He had his toys and he played with them. Bashing the cars together. Bash,

bash. Vroom-vroom. I heard them shouting outside. They didn't like to be bothered when they shouted. When they wanted to shout about my badness.

I wished I could visit my story book. I could walk through a door. There would be a secret place on the other side. My mum would be happy with me. I wouldn't have my evilness inside. Maybe she would hold my hand. Or even smile. Maybe she would want to spend time with me. Maybe my dad didn't be mad all the time and stay with his cheap trollops. I wished I could find a magic door. I didn't know where they were.

Mr. Ted didn't know the way either. Sometimes if me and Mr. Ted closed our eyes we went to a different place. Like pretend. I liked the places in my story books. I wanted to visit the big friendly giant like Sophie. She was an orphan. That made me sad. My Nan said orphans were children whose parents were in heaven. I would be sad if I couldn't see my mum and dad again.

My Nan gave me a story book about a little girl. The little girl didn't have a house. She had matches. She was cold and at the end, her Nan came from heaven and took the little girl with her. It made me sad she was cold and hungry. She watched people have Christmas. If I ever got Christmas presents I would have shared them with the match girl.

I was glad that I had a house and a mum and a dad. I was glad I didn't be an orphan. My mum was the best mum in the whole wide world. I would miss her.

Sometimes when me and Mr. Ted went to magic places the bad man would come. He would make the sky dark. It was a trick so I didn't know where he was. I had to run. Me and Mr. Ted would run our fastest. The bad man always got me. He used his nails and scratched me in my back. It was hard to get away.

My brother tried to get up. He wanted to go to our dad. Our dad always gave him a hug when he came home. My brother wasn't evil like me. He didn't like it when they shouted. They said bad words and used bad names. Then my mum would hit my dad. Then my dad would hit my mum back. My mum would cry and my dad would drink beer from his cans out of the fridge.

I picked up one of my brothers toys. I didn't want him to go outside and be shouted at. He didn't want to play. He wanted to go outside. It was bad to do that. So I grabbed his arm.

Stay here.

Don't go there.

Don't go.

He screamed. Loud. Loud enough to wake the dead maybe. Loud enough to wake the bad man.

My mum stared at me through the window. She had a cigarette in her mouth. Smoke came out of her nose.

Puff, the magic dragon, lived by the sea. I wondered if it felt funny to have smoke in your nose. Maybe it hurt. It didn't seem to hurt my mum, she seemed to like it. My dad would do it on purpose sometimes. Like a game. There was never fire though. Just smoke.

Did it burn?

She raced in so fast. Faster than my dad. Faster than anyone.

"What did you do?" she yelled at me.

I told her nothing. Nothing. Just helping. I moved away. Bad boy all the time. I knew what I had done. I knew I was bad. I moved away. Mustn't give my brother my evilness.

My dad was mad. Bad boy again. The badness always found me.

"Can't you behave for just one day? Is that too much to ask?" he said.

"Tell him properly," my mum said to him. He never told me how she wanted. Maybe that was why it didn't work.

I knew what he was going to say. I knew I had been bad grabbing my brother. I forgot. I wasn't to get my evilness on him.

I could feel my tummy get sick again. I needed to go to the toilet. My head felt fuzzy inside. It was making me tired and I felt hot. Hot under the collar my Nan called it.

My dad picked me up. His hands grabbed me around my arms. He shouted at me loud. I couldn't even hear what he said. My ears hurt.

"Are you listening to me?" he screamed. "You never pay attention. Tell me what I just said."

I couldn't. I didn't know the words. I couldn't hear them. They had been too loud.

"Answer me," he yelled at me.

I told him I didn't know. Told him I couldn't remember. My mum was yelling. She said I didn't listen. That I didn't care. That I didn't want to be part of the family. I did. I really did. I didn't want her to send me away. I just didn't know how to be good.

My dad hit me. He hit me on the side of my face. My ear made a bang inside. He dragged me out of the room. Lifting me in his big strong arms. Then he let go. Dropped me on the ground like I had Mr. Ted. He dropped me on the floor like bricks.

"You're going to stay here until you can tell me what I said. I don't give a damn if it takes you all night. Maybe you also want to think about your behaviour and how you treat everyone," he said.

My dad went back into the back room. I had left Mr. Ted. I had dropped him. I was alone. I didn't know what I would do if the bad man came. Mr. Ted wasn't there to help me. I didn't move from the hall. I sat in the corner and watched the stairs. He was up there. I knew it. Just waiting for me to look away.

I was bad. He would come.

I needed the toilet. It hurted so bad in my tummy. I couldn't ask my dad. I didn't know the words. I couldn't remember.

I tried to think about my story. Like my Nan would say. Think about something nice. My story was nice. Mr. Ted wrote it with me. He helped me like pretend. We wrote about a magic pancake. It made people invisible.

I liked pancakes. I liked when my Nan made them. With sugar and lemons. Lemons made my face feel funny. It must have looked funny because my Nan would laugh.

That was how magic pancakes worked. They had to make your face funny. When you open your eyes. Invisible. I wanted to eat them. Then I could go to school and make people jump.

I would trick my Nan. She would make that funny sound when I jumped out. Then she would laugh and tell me I would get my monkey punched. She always said that. I didn't have a monkey. It sounded funny though. When I would say I don't have a monkey, she would tell me to get on my bike. I didn't have one of those either. I think my Nan liked to play pretend too.

I heard my dad banging in the back room. I didn't know what he was doing. It made me remember I needed the toilet. I didn't dare move. I pulled my legs up close. Tried to make my brain remember the words.

It was too late. The badness got me. It made me not hold it anymore. The floor under me got wet. I didn't dare move.

My dad was going to be mad.

Mr Ted.

Why do I be so bad all the time? I don't mean to do it. It happens. I'm so bad. Maybe they should make me live somewhere else and then I don't make them sad. I'm sorry. I'm sorry. I'm sorry.

## SEVEN

*Little boy, little boy*
*Sat here in the hall,*
*Your Dad is coming,*
*Curl up like a ball.*

My legs felt invisible. But I could see them. They were still there. Naked and cold. They didn't feel like they were there. If I closed my eyes maybe they disappeared. Like magic. Maybe I couldn't walk on them anymore. Maybe I would be like my Gaga and have to use a stick.

My Gaga was in heaven. It made my Nan sad that he was there. She missed him. I tried to make her smile, but she was still sad. He was funny. He talked funny. He used words that I didn't think were real. I liked the way he talked. I tried to copy it but I couldn't. Maybe it was a secret language. He used it when he talked to someone called Allah. He said Allah was like God.

Maybe he was with God or Allah in heaven. He went to heaven after I had got to kiss him night-night him my mum said. Gaga had told me about heaven. He said when he was there he could see me, but I couldn't see him. I wished he would tell the bad man to not come back. Gaga told me if I talked to him he could hear me. Me and Mr. Ted would say night-night to him. Like we did before he went to heaven.

In the morning, I would say Good Morning, Mr. Hedgehog. It was a song from school. It made me think of my Gaga.

It was nearly dark time when I was still sat in the hallway. Maybe the bad man would come soon because I was alone. My dad hadn't come out. I knew the bad man would come because I had been bad too much. I didn't have anything to make it hurt myself. I told the bad man I was sorry. But Mr. Ted was in the back room and he couldn't tell the bad man for me.

The carpet was still wet. My dad came out. I squeezed myself together. I hoped he wouldn't see the floor. He would be mad at me. He looked at me with his mad eyes. I put my head down. I felt bad. I was bad inside. I didn't want him to see. I didn't want him to shout at me.

"Well?" he said.

I didn't know. I couldn't remember the words still. Maybe he would make me sit in the hallway forever and ever. Maybe he would if he saw the carpet. My mum came into the hallway. She didn't look at me. It was time for my brother's bath and bed time. She carried him up the stairs and played with him. I wished my mum loved me like that. I wished I could be good enough like my brother. Maybe when I was good she would give me a hug.

Only my Nan gave me hugs. But it made my mum mad if she saw. I liked my Nan's hugs. She made me feel warm.

I didn't look at my mum. I knew if she saw I would get told off. I wasn't good enough to look at her when I was bad.

My dad told me to stand up. My legs felt funny inside. Maybe they had been sleeping. They did that sometimes when I was made to stand in the corner.

My dad pulled me forwards by my arms. My feet felt like they were fat. They didn't look fat. I wondered if my dad thought they were, but I didn't ask him.

"Do you not know how to use the bathroom?" he asked me.

I said I didn't know in my head. I told my dad that the bad man would be upstairs. But I didn't say the words. I didn't want my dad to fight the bad man and get hurt.

"Why? All the time. You just can't behave can you? I come in from work and I have to deal with this all the time," he yelled at me. He used bad words I wasn't allowed to say and names that made me feel sad inside.

He told me to get into the god damn kitchen and get the mess cleaned up before my mum saw. I did. Even if my legs didn't want to walk. They tingled inside.

Mr. Ted was on the table in the back room. I stopped and whispered to him. I told him I was sorry and could he please tell the bad man I was sorry too. I hoped I hadn't hurt him when I dropped him. I hoped my dad didn't be mad at him. It wasn't Mr. Ted's fault. I hoped he would still be my friend.

I put the bucket in the sink in the kitchen. And turned the hot tap on. I put my hand in the water like my mum did to see if it was warm. I didn't move my hand when it got hot. I didn't want to. It stung and made my skin pink. I just watched it. The bucket filled all the way over the top and into the sink. It made the bubbles float away, but I couldn't help it. My teacher said I was a daydreamer. I liked to go to places in my brain.

I didn't hear my dad come in. I had been in a place far, far away. He pushed me out of the way and I nearly fell over. My tummy tickled because he made me jump.

"Do you think that I just have money that I can pour down the drain?" He asked.

I shook my head. Shook it so hard maybe it would fall off. Like Worzel Gummidge. He could change his head. Maybe I needed a new head. One that was good. Maybe I could ask the crowman for one. I would have to think about it when I saw him on the television.

I didn't moan. Didn't make a sound. Didn't move. Quiet. Still.

My mum came in. She had heard my dad yelling at me. Heard I had been bad again. He told her. Told her about the disgusting boy that used the floor as the toilet. She said I wasn't good enough to use the one in the house. If I wanted to use the floor I could go outside.

Down the bottom of the garden with the spiders and the bugs and the creepy crawlies. I had to use the outside toilet. I didn't get to put no shoes on. The stones hurt my feet. Better than the tingles. I needed my legs invisible again.

My dad standed outside while I went to the toilet. I didn't get to shut the door because there was no light. It was dark when the door closed and my dad said he didn't want to have to come in and get me if I got scared.

Then we went back into the house. My mum cleaned my mess. She didn't talk to me. I said night-

night to her. Maybe she didn't hear me. I made my hand squeeze my arms. I squeezed hard. Hard so it hurt. I didn't cry. I was too bad to cry. I didn't get to cry or I would get something to cry about.

My dad told me to go to the bathroom. I didn't get my own water. I had to use my brother's. It was little and cold and grey. I didn't talk. My dad didn't either. He wasn't my friend. He would be mad if I asked him for more water.

I wished I could be good. I didn't mean to go to the toilet on the carpet. I didn't mean to get sick on the floor. My tummy growled. It sounded like scary frogs in my tummy. I didn't ask my dad about food. I only got that when I was good.

My dad got the cup. He filled it with water from inside the bath and tipped it on my head. It was cold. I closed my eyes.

He got the soap and made me stand up. It didn't made bubbles like my mum's soap did. It smelled funny too. Like the road stuff outside.

He put the soap all over me and then he put the soap down there on my private parts. He kept his hand there and squeezed tight. I thought he might hurt me like the bad man did because I had not used the toilet.

I was scared. I wanted him to let go. I tried not to cry about it because it made me frightened in my tummy. My dad didn't hurt me. He let go and told me to go and get in the bedroom.

I didn't get a towel. I dripped like the clothes on the washing line. My dad closed the door.

The bad man couldn't come if my dad was in there and the door was closed. My dad made me stand by the wall. I thought he was going to make me stand there all night. He knelt behind me and put his hand down there again. He put his other hand on his own thing. I think he was mad. He breathed like he did when he was going to shout.

His wee got on my leg. I wondered why he didn't use the toilet. Then he got up and told me to get dressed and sit on the box. He went downstairs and left me alone.

Mr Ted.

I wish I got to be good. I was a bad boy and I went to the toilet on the floor. My Daddy did it too. But he didn't get any told off. Why do I be bad all the time?

## EIGHT

Little boy, little boy
It's a brand new day
Wake up now, wake up,
Go and be on your way

The bad man didn't come that night. I waited for him. Waited and waited until my eyes got too tired. I didn't get a blanket. I was bad for that. But my dad did bring me Mr. Ted. Maybe Mr. Ted annoyed them like I do.

I lay on the box. Opened the curtains and window. I wasn't allowed the light on. There wasn't one in the roof anyway. Just a lamp by the bed. But I didn't get to turned it on. My mum said it wasted the money. I opened the window so if the bad man came then someone could hear me. No one ever heard me when I shouted. And I shouted as loud as I could. My mum never heard me.

Then my mum and dad came to bed. They didn't say night-night to me. I stayed on the box. They didn't talk to me. I tried so hard to be brave when I lied there. A brave little boy like in the stories. Boys in books were always brave. Not like me. I was scared. Scardey cat most of the time. I hugged Mr. Ted on the box. My tears kept coming. I tried not to let them, but it just happened. Like my evilness.

I hid my face behind Mr. Ted. I didn't get to cry for my mum. She said I couldn't cry over my evilness. "It is a part of how you were made," she would say. "We do not feel pity for what we are, we just change it." I didn't know how to change it. I wished I could. I wished I could make everything better.

I couldn't stop the crying. I could feel my evilness where my heart was. It scrunched up. I wished I could hug my mum. I wished she would hug me like she did my brother. Maybe then it would all go away. I wished I could be a good boy.

I lay and watched my mum and dad in the dark. Maybe if I got invisible they would be happy. They wouldn't fight any more. I watched all night until the moon went to sleep. I wondered whose bed it went under in the light time. My dad said the moon liked to sleep under beds. I watched as the sun got up. It made me think of the sun having a hat. I had never seen it with a hat. Except in pictures. Maybe it would be too hot and set the hat on fire.

My dad waked up. He sat and smoked a cigarette as he put on his jeans and boots. I didn't know if I could go downstairs. I didn't ask. Didn't know if I was allowed.

My mum got out of bed. She told me to get dressed for school. I had a uniform. It was too small for me. She had got it at a jumble sale because she didn't have much money. The school said I had to have it. "The school should buy these damned things, at these prices." She said.

I couldn't take Mr. Ted to school with me. I left him by the window so he could look out for when I came home again. I went downstairs. There was no breakfast on the table for me. I was too scared to ask. I didn't like when they said no. It made me feel sad inside. It was bad to ask for food. My mum said it was begging.

"You'll get fed when you've earned the right to sit at this table," she told me.

I went to the kitchen. My mum hadn't told me to, but I got myself on the stool ready. Every day was my medicine. To take away the devil from my brain, my mum told me. So the evil would go away. So I sat and waited.

"Did I tell you, you could sit?" she asked when she came into the kitchen.

I tried to get off. My mum ran over and pulled me off. She threw me so I fell at the fridge. Like a heap. A great big heap on her floor. I had to stand fast or I would be in trouble for that too.

When I tried to stand my mum stared at me. I didn't like it when she did that. Her eyes looked mad at me and I didn't know what to do. I wished she would tell me so I wouldn't get in trouble all the time. Maybe she could give me a list.

She gave me my medicine. From my cow cup. The cup with no cow on it anymore. I opened my mouth. She didn't bash my tooth. I ate it and pretended I was George. He got magic medicine. It made magic things happen. His medicine was marvellous. If mine was ever magic I wanted it to make me fly. Like Superman . He could fly. I tried to practice my flying, but I never jumped off the floor enough. Maybe only really good boys got to be like Superman . Maybe it was because I didn't have a cape. I asked Santa for one. But he never gived me one. I used a blanket instead.

My medicine made my tummy sick. It made my neck hot inside and my eyes water. Not crying though. I wasn't crying, water just came from them. Like they were leaking because I was too hot. My mum picked me up off the floor and pushed me outside. She opened the back gate and I tried to get my sick in the gutter. Not in my shoes though. She didn't want the smell in her house. "I'll be smelling that shit all day," she said.

I didn't be allowed to go back into the house after. Just in case I got sick again. I had to go right to school. It wasn't far away. Just along two alleyways. I always crossed with the lollypop lady. She was nice, but she didn't speak to me a lot. I think she knew that

I was bad. My mum used to tell her things and she would shake her head about it.

My mum said she was a nosey old bat. My Nan was one of those too. Except my mum used bad words. Ones that I wasn't allowed to say. I wondered what a nosey old bat was. It made me think of witches. They turned into bats sometimes. I didn't think my Nan or the Lollypop lady was a witch.

When I got to school I sat and watched everyone play. I wished I could play. But they were all friends. They didn't like me. Maybe they knew I was evil inside. I just sat and watched them. Maybe one day one of them would ask me to play. I was sure I would say yes. I would be on my best behaviour. Like my Nan said I had to do when we were out at her friend's house.

Mr Ted.

I am just bad. I wish I could go away.

# DEAR TEDDY

## NINE

Little boy, little boy
You've banged your knee,
Cover it up fast,
Don't let her see.

I liked school. I got to read lots of books. My teacher let me get books from the library. Sometimes I thought I could sit there all day.

I liked to pretend. Mr. Ted liked pretend too. My mum said pretend was for liars.

I didn't like play time. I didn't get any friends. I just sat and waited to go in again. Lunch-time was okay. I got to eat lots. If I ate the fastest they called for seconds. Lots of days I got seconds on my lunch.

I could stay inside a long time when I got seconds. It was cold outside. I didn't have a coat. My mum said she would buy one when she had some more money. I didn't mind. I had never really had a coat. My brother had two coats. He wore one and hugged one. He didn't have a Mr. Ted like me. So he hugged a red coat. No one took it off him. He cried if it was gone.

When school was over my mum met me at the shop near school. She always waited there. Her friend was the shop keeper. I thought maybe she was rich. She was my mum's friend. They would talk and have coffee.

I walked from school to the shop. It was one road. Straight line my mum said. No reason for me to get lost.

I walked between the parked cars. Like a secret spy. Like James Bond. Hiding. I didn't get to see the brick that was by the drain. I caught my shoe and fell over. My knee bashed on the ground. It made it bleed.

I didn't cry. My eyes tried. But I made it go away. I didn't want to be a spy after that. I didn't want to fall down again. Spies didn't fall down. Spies didn't cry. Spies didn't be bad like me. I always got things wrong.

My mum was at the shop. She was talking and smoking a cigarette. I had to stand still next to my mum. I watched the blood from my knee go down my leg. It was like a snake. When I moved my leg, more blood came out. My mum didn't see. She was too busy. They talked about boring things. If I had a friend, I wanted to talk to him about good things. Like I did Mr. Ted. Maybe he would like to play pretend with me too.

A girl from my class came into the shop. She didn't talk to me. She was with her mum. She asked her mum for sweets and her mum said yes. She got a paper bag and filled it with lots of sweets. Then her mum gave my mum's friend some pennies and the girl ate the sweets. The girl started to eat them. I wondered what they tasted like. I didn't get sweets often. Just when my Nan got them for me. I never asked my mum for them. She would be mad because I was too bad.

I wondered what the girl was like. She had to be very good to get sweets. I wondered if she got frightened at night. Maybe because she was good enough for sweets there was no bad man. The girl left. When my mum finished talking we left too.

I think my mum knew everyone in the whole wide world. I walked behind her. She said hello to everyone. Even the lollypop lady stopped to say hello. Nosey old bat.

She looked down at my leg. Then she told my mum and my mum looked down at my leg too.

"Why didn't you say anything?" she asked me. I shrugged my shoulders. I didn't know why. I couldn't say. I was just bad. Bad inside all the time. Even when I tried to be good it happened. Even when I was just playing. I fell and I got bad again. All the time. Such a bad boy.

That's all it was. We walked to the house. My mum was mad. She walked fast. When we got to the house I stood at the gate. "I'm sorry," I said. My tummy hurt. It always hurt when I knew she was going to be mad at me.

"If you're sorry you wouldn't have done it," she said.

"It was on accident," I said.

We went into the house. Into the kitchen. She told me to take my shoes and socks off. I did.

She put my sock under the tap. She used some cleaning powder. I didn't know what it was. She cleaned everything with it. My dad used it to clean the oil from his hands at night.

She was mad. She rubbed the sock and said bad words out loud. I wished I didn't play pretend and fell. Then my mum wouldn't be mad at the mess I made.

"This is never going to come out," she said. "I'll have to tell your father about this. It's another pair of socks gone. More money down the swanny."

My mum got the dish cloth. She put it under the hot tap. Then she got the cleaning powder and put it on the cloth. It smelled like lemon. She told me to sit on the stool. I did. She told me to put my leg out. I did that too.

She put the cloth on my knee. It burned like fire. I cried. My mum grabbed my leg and held it in place. I tried to pull my leg away. I shouted at her. She shouted back at me. She called me bad names and told me to keep my damn leg in place if I knew what was good for me.

She told me to stop crying. She pointed her finger at me. She had her face at mine. I bited my teeth. I tried to stop the crying. She put the cloth on my leg again. I thought my leg was going to cut off. It hurt so much. I couldn't keep the crying away. My mum cleaned my leg. I got off the stool. My leg hurt so bad.

"You're bad mum," I said to her.

She came to me. She put her face at mine. I sat on the floor. By the vacuum. I made myself into a ball.

"I'm what?" she shouted. "What did you say?"

I shook my head.

"Say it," she said.

"Bad," I whispered. "You hurted my leg."

I didn't mean her to be mad. I wished she was sorry. Like when I hurt someone else. I had to be sorry. If she was sorry she would hug me like when I tried to be sorry. Then I could tell her no like she did. Because that's what happens when your bad. No one gets to hug you.

She told me to go up to the bedroom. To get up there and not dare make a sound. I didn't want to go there. I had been bad. The bad man would come. I told her I was sorry.

She pulled my arm and made me stand up. She walked me through the backroom to the hallway. She pointed at the stairs.

My tummy needed to be sick and to go to the toilet. I was afraid. I didn't want to go upstairs. The bad man would come. My mum wouldn't hear me shout and he would get me. He always did when I was bad.

She shouted at me. I didn't want her to shout. He would hear. He would know.

I checked everywhere with my eyes when I went upstairs. I didn't want him to jump out. He liked to do that it and made me more scared. I checked with my ears. Maybe I could hear him move.

Mr. Ted was still on the box. I sat with him and opened the bedroom window. I told Mr. Ted about how bad I was. I told Mr. Ted I had been sent to the bedroom and to please keep the bad man away.

My mum was going to make me stay in the bedroom forever. I kept watching the door so he couldn't sneaked up on me.

Mr Ted.

I wish I knew how to do things right. Maybe then my Mummy didn't get mad at me all the time. Maybe then she would give me a hug and make it better.

## TEN

*Little boy, little boy*
*Pretend you're not here*
*It'll be over soon*
*There's nothing to fear.*

I didn't get to turn the lamp on. I didn't get any light from the hall landing. It got dark outside. I tried to be quiet. Tried to be still and not make any noise.

I hugged Mr. Ted. It was cold outside. I was cold inside. Inside my skin. But I kept the window open just in case. I didn't get to shout very loud in the house. Maybe someone outside would hear me.

The open window made me shiver. My teeth chattered together. If I let my voice out I could make noises with my shiver. Like a tune. My mum told me off when I did that.

I watched as my dad came home. He had a giant motorbike. I wanted a bike like his. He was clever. He made it himself. My mum said he loved his bike more than his family. My dad said it was to escape nagging. I didn't know what a nagging was. I had never seen it.

His bike made a giant noise. Like a monster growling really loud. I told Mr. Ted when we were big. We would make a bike. Mr. Ted could sit at the front.

I knew my mum was going to tell my dad about my badness. I knew that he was going to be mad at me for it. I hugged Mr. Ted tight. I rested my face on his head and whispered I was sorry.

I had been on my box forever. My mum brought my brother upstairs. I listened when she put him in bed. She said night-night to him. She did not talk to me. I waited for her to come in. I watched the door. Maybe she wouldn't be mad at me anymore. But she was.

My mum was going to church. I didn't know what kind of church. She said it wasn't like normal ones. She got to talk to ghosts. She said that she had talked to my Gaga. I wondered if they talked to monsters. Maybe things that hid in the dark. Like the bad man. She could tell him I was trying to get better.

She said the church made her better. She had been sick. The sickness had made her hurt my big brother. He didn't live with us. The bad people had taken him away. The sickness made her throw my big brother at the fire. But she was sorry. It was on accident. No one listened and they gave him to a new mum and dad. It made my mum sad. My Nan said not to ask because it made my mum sad. I didn't want to make her sad.

My mum said if I didn't get to be good I would have to leave too. Maybe I wouldn't get a new mum and dad. Bad boys stayed in homes with no food. They didn't get to see their mum and dad again. I tried my bestest to be good so I didn't get sent away. I wished my mum's cure would work. It took forever and ever to get better.

When my mum went out, my dad came upstairs. He came into the bedroom and put the lamp on. Me and Mr. Ted remembered how everyone's feet walked. We knew it was my dad. We shut the window before he came in. He would be mad. He would tell my mum. She would be mad too. Then my dad would have to shout at me.

My dad gave me a bowl. It had bananas and custard in. It was cold from dinner. But I liked it that way. I ate it all up.

He asked me why I didn't tell my mum about my knee. I said I didn't know.

He sat on the bed with his drink. When he finished it all up and I finished my bananas and custard he took the bowl and glass downstairs.

He came back upstairs again. I thought it might be his bed time. It was dark outside. I was still in my school clothes. No one had said to get changed. Sometimes they didn't say. So I slept in my day clothes. But my dad told me to go to the bathroom. He told me to brush my teeth and use the toilet. I told him it was dark. I was frightened.

My dad stood on the landing while I used the bathroom. I used it my fastest. I didn't want my dad to go away. Then the bad man could come and get me. But not when my dad stood there. He was big and strong.

I didn't feel very well. My neck hurt when I swallowed. I was cold. Cold on the inside. I felt tired. Like my head was sleepy. I didn't ask to go to bed. I sat on my box again. I hugged Mr. Ted. I tried to keep my shivers away. My skin prickled. It maked my eyes wanted to sleep.

My dad had made me a drink just like his. But it was warm. He said it had honey in. It would make me feel better. I wanted to show Mr. Ted. My dad had shared his special drink with me. It made me happy inside. I didn't tell my dad I didn't like it. Maybe he would shout and yell at me. I didn't want him to take it away. I put my fingers around it. The glass was warm. It made my hands warm too.

It made me warm inside when I drank it.

My dad told me to stand up. He lifted my arms up and pulled off my top. I was cold. He put my pyjama top on me. But it didn't make me warm. He changed my shorts too. I thought I had to get on my box again. But my dad said to get in bed. It was cold in there so he turned on the hot blanket that plugged into the wall.

He got in bed with me. I got to lie on his arm. I felt warm with my dad there behind me. The bad man couldn't come. I wished I could stay there all night.

My dad had a book. I didn't ever get read to. I heard him read to my brother. I liked his voice when he read. It made me sleepy.

My dad read to me and Mr. Ted. I hugged Mr. Ted. My dad held my hand as he read. He got my hand and moved it behind me. He put my hand on his thing.

I didn't know why. He kissed my ear and whispered to me. He whispered the book words. His hand was over mine. He read the book about a thing called a Hobbit. It was his eleventy first birthday. My dad made my hand move up and down.

The Hobbit was getting a party for his birthday. I didn't know how many birthdays eleventy first was. My pyjamas got wet. I wondered if my dad wet the bed. But only babies wet the bed. My dad wasn't a baby.

He moved my hand back and hugged me. I hugged Mr. Ted. We fell asleep with my dad.

## DEAR TEDDY

Dear Mr Ted.

    I did something with my Daddy today. I don't know what it is. I didn't like it. Please ask him not to do it again. It maked me feel funny.

## ELEVEN

Little boy, little boy
Sick on the floor
She'll beat you, she'll smack you
She doesn't care anymore.

I didn't remember my mum coming home. When I waked up she was in bed. My dad was gone. He had got up already. I could hear him downstairs.

I didn't feel very well. I wanted to go back to sleep. My eyes felt sleepy. I got out of bed. My mum would be mad if I stayed there. I had to go to school. I was cold on the inside still. Maybe Jack Frost had come and frozen me. My knees and legs felt like they were frozen inside. They were hard to move.

I went downstairs to find my dad. He made me breakfast. But I didn't want any. I was too tired and cold. I couldn't breathe. I wanted to lay my head on the table and go to sleep. But I knew it was bad manners. I didn't get to put my arms on the table. I didn't think heads was allowed too. Maybe Mr. Ted would sleep with me. Maybe we could sleep outside. Like Stig, the man that lived in the dump. I hoped Mr. Ted didn't get sick too. I didn't know how to fix sick teddy bears.

My dad gave me porridge. Not a lot. I asked for a little bit. I asked for extra sugar because my mouth made my breakfast taste funny. My dad sat at the table with me. He had a giant mug. He drank tea.

My dad said that on the weekend he was going to the library. He said I could go if I wanted to. He said I could pick out some books. I had to be good. We could read them together. I had never been to the library with my dad. He said it was giant. He said my eyes would pop out of my head. I wondered if it was bigger than the one at school.

"Six books you can get," he said to me.

Maybe my eyes already popped from my head. I didn't have a mirror so I couldn't look. I promised my dad that I would be on my bestest behaviour. I wouldn't make my mum mad at me. I would tell Mr. Ted to tell the bad man that I was going to be good this week. No badness.

I promise.

I promise

Then me and Mr. Ted could see a giant library. Maybe they had giant books too. Mr. Ted would be excited in his tummy. I was going to be so good.

My mum came down with my brother. My dad gave him food too. My dad kissed my mum goodbye and then he kissed my brother. Then he went to work.

His big giant motorbike growled in the alley way. It growled all the way down the road. Like a monster running away.

My mum took my bowl. I wasn't finished. Some of the porridge spilled on the table when I tried to let go of my spoon. Sticky white mess. I cleaned it up with my hand before she saw.

"Kitchen," she said.

I went in the kitchen. My nose kept sniffing. My mum gave me a tissue and told me to blow it. "Are you ill?" she asked.

I shrugged my shoulders. She gave me some medicine from a bottle in the cupboard. It tasted like strawberries. I liked that medicine. Maybe she could make her medicine taste like strawberries too.

She made my other medicine in my cow cup. It was more runny than the day before. Runny and sticky and orange. I wondered if it tasted like oranges.

Strawberries and orange for medicine.

She put the spoon in my mouth. It nearly made my mouth explode. Maybe my eyes did pop out of my head again. I couldn't breathe. She held my mouth shut to stop the medicine coming out because my lips didn't want to close. My tongue burnt down my neck. It was hot and I wanted to cough. I couldn't cough because my mum had hold of my mouth.

My neck hurt so much. I coughed nearly some more. It was like hot snot in my nose. It made my eyes cry again.

My mum told me to sit on the stool. She went to the back door and smoked a cigarette. My brother came in the kitchen. He had finished his food. He had a toy. He wanted to play. He put his car on my knee. I watched it when it rolled onto the floor. He picked it up and put it back. I let it roll off again. I didn't want to play. I wasn't allowed to play.

He tried to give it to me again. In my hands. I pushed it away. He laughed and tried again. I don't know why I did it. It was my badness. I kicked him. He fell on the floor and cried. I was sorry.

My mum saw. She ran and pulled me so hard with my arm maybe she was going to fling me away. She pulled my pyjama pants down and slapped my legs. I couldn't stop it, the sickness in my tummy. It came out and made me jump. It landed on my feet. It landed on my mum's feet. She was mad with me.

The sick made my mum let go. She dropped me to the ground and stepped back. She picked my brother up and took him into the back room. I sat in my sick. I hugged my tummy and cried because I didn't feel well. I cried because I had been bad and my dad wouldn't take me to the library. And I cried because it scrunched up inside.

My mum came back in the kitchen. She didn't shout. She didn't smack me. She didn't talk. I didn't move. I knew she would be more mad if I made more mess. I couldn't be bad more. I was bad enough.

She went to the kitchen sink and filled a bucket it with water. She got the cleaning powder and tipped some in the water. Then she came to me and told me to stand up. I did. She took off my pyjamas. She put them in the bucket and used them to clean the floor too.

Then she filled the sink with water and cleaning powder. The sink was big. It was like a bath. She picked me up. I tried to wriggle. The water was too hot. It hurt my feet and my legs. I screamed and cried. I tried to pick my feet up. I tried to get away from the water.

She told me to shut up. She said that I had to stop making a noise because I would disturb the neighbours. She got my cow cup and filled it with water. She poured it down my legs. I screamed at her. She slapped me and told me to stop it. I put my hands on my face to squash away the scream. I squeezed my fingers on my face. Maybe I could pull it off.

When I was clean my mum lifted me out of the sink. My skin was all red. I told my mum I hated her. I told her that I wasn't her friend any more. I said it over lots of times. I wanted her to be sad. I wanted her to cry that I wasn't her friend. I wanted her to be sorry. I said it lots and lots, but she didn't get sad.

She told me to get in the back room. I did. She gave me some clothes and told me to get them on. I wasn't going to school. I had to sit by the fire and the chair and not make a sound. I didn't want to talk to her. She was naughty. Naughtier than me.

My Nan came at dinner time to help my mum and My mum told her about my badness. My Nan looked at me. She was sad my badness had come out. My mum told my Nan what I had said. My Nan said I shouldn't say things like that to my mum. She said hate was a bad word and I should never use it.

She said maybe I should say sorry to my mum. I didn't want to. I didn't talk to my Nan. I folded my arms and looked at the floor. My mum was bad. I wanted her to be sorry. Maybe if I didn't talked to her she would feel bad and come and talked to me.

I waited forever. She didn't get sorry. I didn't like not being my mum's friend. I went into the kitchen. She was washing the plates. I told her I was sorry. I tried to hug her. But she took my arms away and told me not to touch her.

"Get your filthy hands off me," she said.

I went back in the back room and sat by the fire. I hugged Mr. Ted with my filthy hands.
Mr Ted.

My Mummy isn't my friend today. I got my evilness and it got mad at her. I didn't mean to do it. Please tell her I'm sorry. I'll be good forever and ever.

## TWELVE

Little boy, little boy,
The bad mans near
Don't scream, don't cry
No one will hear.

I wished I had got to go to school. Just for the lunch time. Then I could have got seconds. My tummy got excited thinking about it. But I had to tell it we weren't going. I asked Mr. Ted if he was hungry too. He didn't get no breakfast or lunch. I don't think Mr. Ted got sad about it. Mr. Ted could eat pretend food. I wished I could eat pretend food. I would eat the biggest pancake in the world.

My Nan made me a sandwich. It had strawberry jam on it. When I squished the bread together it came out at the sides. I licked it with my fingers and got them all sticky. My mum didn't get to see. She would be mad. I was making a mess. I didn't share the jam with Mr. Ted. It made his fur sticky.

My brother got to play. My mum went to work. Sometimes she went to the hotel and made the bedrooms all nice. Then she would go swimming. My Nan stayed with us. I was too tired to talk. I fell asleep on the floor. I didn't get to use the chairs. I wasn't allowed on them. My brother had his own special chair. Sometimes I sat on it when no one was at home. Then no one could see. Except the bad man. He could read minds. I would remember when I sat on the chair. I would say sorry and get on the floor again.

My mum came back from the hotel. She cleaned up. My Nan went home again. I didn't remember her going. I was sleeping a lot. Mr. Ted said goodbye to her though. She gave us both a kiss before she went. She always kissed Mr. Ted. I hoped she didn't get none of her pink lipstick in his fur. He was a boy. Boys don't wear makeup.

My dad never came home for dinner that day. My mum said on the phone to her friend that he was out. "No doubt jumping some cheap tart while I slave away looking after his children," she said. She puffed her cigarette when she talked. It made the smoke come out in clouds. I watched them as they went up in the air. Like the caterpillar in Alice of wonderland. He could make circles with his smoke. Maybe my mum could. I had seen my dad do it. I tried to catch them, but they just went away.

My mum gave my brother some dinner. He sat at the table and watched the cartoons. He had toast and egg and spaghetti hoops. I liked eggs and soldiers best. I liked when the egg was all runny inside. My dad made the best eggs. If I got to be good sometimes he would give me two. I could eat the whole box. I would share them with Mr. Ted though.

I stayed sleeping on the floor. My mum gave me some of the medicine from the bottle. The strawberry one. Not the orange one. Because it wasn't really oranges and it wasn't for my nose. It was for my badness.

It was dark. She bathed my brother and put him in bed. She told me to go upstairs and get changed and to get in her bed.

I wished I had my own bed like my brother. He got to have pictures on his bed. His bed was little.

## DEAR TEDDY

It had been his cot before. A baby cot. But he wasn't a baby any more so my dad took the sides off and made it into a little bed for him. I liked to lie in it and read to him. But I didn't get to do that a lot. My mum didn't like me near him in case he caught my evilness. I didn't want my brother to get evil. Or have my badness.

I was scared to get changed. I took Mr. Ted. He could hold my hand. I didn't want to tell my mum I was scared. She would get mad at me for it. She would call me names that made me feel silly inside. I didn't like it when she did that. She spoke funny. Her voice made me sad inside.

My mum didn't tell me to get in bed. So I sat on my box with Mr. Ted. I wanted to go back to sleep. My nose was all full. I had to breathe from my mouth. It made my neck inside hurt more. Every time I blowed my nose. It just filled some more. But my mum told me off for making sniff noises. I didn't get to do it on purpose.

When my mum came in the bedroom. She told me to get into bed. I did. I got in at the side near the door. It was the only side I was allowed on. She lifted my pyjama top and told me she has some medicine to make me breathe better.

It was warm. It made my skin tingle. Like it was humming. It smelled funny. I didn't like the smell. It made me think of the bad man. The smell made my eyes sleepy. My mum's hand was cold. But I wanted to fall asleep.

I didn't hear the bad man come in. I didn't know my mum had gone. I didn't know how. It was like magic. I screamed for my mum. I didn't bother to get in trouble for waking my brother. The bad man was there. I tried so hard to shout. I couldn't make my voice hard enough.

The bad man pulled at my covers. I tried to hold onto them. He was too strong for me. He was big and I couldn't do it. I shouted for my mum. But she didn't hear. I didn't fall asleep this time. I always fell asleep when the bad man came.

I didn't get any clothes on. My mum had just left my underwear. The bad man pushed me down. He digged his fingers into my shoulders with his nails. He bent down and bited me. He bit my shoulder. I tried to scream, but he squashed me and I couldn't. He squashed my shout away. He was too heavy. He kept biting. Lots and lots. It hurt and I cried. My arms were stuck. He was holding them. He pushed me up the bed.

My head hitted the wall. It was hard. It made my brain hurt inside. My ears made a funny noise. It was loud. My head hurt so bad.

The bad man climbed on me. He put his knees on my arms and sat on me. His knees squashed my arms. He was going to snap them.

He opened his pants. And took his thing out. I didn't want to do what I had done with my dad. I didn't like it. I tried to get the bad man off. I tried to call for my mum. I didn't get anyone to hear me.

He pushed it at my face. I turned my head away. I was sorry for kicking my brother. It was on accident. I was never going to be bad like that again.

He put his hand on my neck. My head bashed the wall again. It made me dizzy. I wanted my Mr. Ted.

I wanted my mum.

His hand squeezed my neck. It made me hurt inside. I couldn't breathe. My nose was still filled up. But it was running down my face with the crying. It made my lips feel slimy. I couldn't get my arms up and I couldn't breathe.

He banged my head again. I cried. My mouth got open and he pushed it in there. Like my mum did with the spoon. He nearly made it go down my neck. He kept trying to push it down. I tried to shout for my mum. My mouth was too full. I couldn't breathe. My head was going to pop. My mouth was going to break open like it did at the dentist.

Something yucky tasted in my neck. Something squeezed in. It squeezed to the back of my neck. It made me want to cough. I couldn't cough because the bad man was there and it didn't stop. Like when my mum made me not cough and the cough came in my nose.

He got off me. I got sick. I didn't get to stop it. I curled on my side. The bad man left. I cried and got sick. I didn't shout my mum. She would be mad at me. She would make me sleep on the box. She would put me in the hot water with the cleaning powder. My mouth was dirty inside. From the sick and the bad man.

I put my pillow on the sick. Then my mum didn't see when she got to bed. My feet hooked together. I didn't know where Mr. Ted was. I hoped he was okay. I hugged my arms. I put my hands under my chin. I squeezed at the bites from the bad man.

I rocked to go to sleep. When I squeezed the bited part it banged in my skin. It helped me rock. I fell asleep.

Mr Ted.

Please don't let the bad man get me again. Please keep him away. I won't ever be bad. I won't. I'm sorry.

## THIRTEEN

Little boy, little boy
It's just your dad,
Be good for him, promise
Please don't be bad.

On the weekend I did get to go to the library. I got to be good all week. My mum didn't shout at my sick in the bed. She made me get in the bath. The water got cold before I got in. It made me shiver. It made my teeth do their shake.

Then she gave me some hot pop. It tasted like blackcurrant. It was sweet. It made me warm inside. The smell was scratchy in my nose. It was better in my mouth. My mouth felt dirty inside. I tried to brush it away. I brushed hard with my tooth brush. I even made my teeth bleed. It didn't make it no better.

I got the sick in my tummy again. I didn't tell my mum. I did it in the toilet. She didn't see. I cleaned it off the seat. She didn't need to get mad at me for it. I was a good boy. I would be a good boy. Mr. Ted could tell the bad man I wouldn't be bad ever again. Then he wouldn't need to put his thing in my mouth.

When I got bathed and drank my hot pop I got in bed. My mum put whole pyjamas on me. Ones with pants and a top. Like ones that my brother got. They were too big for me. Got to hide my hands in the sleeves. The bed was all clean. The bedroom smelled like the cleaning powder.

When my mum put me in bed. My dad came home. I heard his motorbike growl. Maybe he would make me sleep on the box because of my badness. He came upstairs. He was smoking a cigarette. He took his clothes off and got into bed. My mum got in too. I slept in the middle. It was warm. The bad man could not come with both of them there.

My dad put his hand in my pyjama pants. But he didn't do anything like before. He just kept his hand there for a little bit. I hugged Mr. Ted. We didn't mind. My dad hugged me. He made me warm inside. I fell asleep.

I got to be good the rest of the week. I got mashed potato with baked beans one night. I had been on my bested behaviour. I tried so hard. When my mum gave me my medicine. I sat like a good boy and waited. She didn't get mad. I didn't get sick on the floor. She didn't need to shout at me.

The bad man only came one more time. But I fell asleep again that time. He didn't do the same. Maybe I had not been bad like before. Maybe it was just because of my bad thoughts. When the bad man had been. I waked up after. It was dark. The covers were tucked in all around. Even my head. I couldn't breathe. I was upside down in bed like a bat. Mr. Ted was at the pillow.

I shouted for my mum. She would hear me. Maybe the bad man's magic went away and she heard me. Sometimes I lied there listening. Maybe he was still there. His face was scary. He had big yellow eyes. His face always smiled. Like a monster.

My mum came to take the covers off. I couldn't breathe. I cried because it was hot and I couldn't move. I told my mum about the man. She said that it was the demon. He came because I was bad. The evilness inside made him come. She said that she had a picture of him. She said she would show me if I wanted. I didn't want to see his picture. I didn't want to see his eyes. He made me frightened inside.

I wished I could get invisible and go away. Then he wouldn't find me. Maybe Mr. Ted could tell him I was gone and he would leave me alone. I didn't want him to get my brother instead. My brother had to be good.

When it was Saturday I got out of bed. I got dressed. Ate all my breakfast right up and waited for my medicine. I didn't get the sick on the floor. When I had my cure. I sat outside and waited for my dad. He worked in the morning. He said to be ready or he would go without me. I waited and waited.

Inside my tummy got happy when I heard his monster bike. I heard it a long time before I could see him. I didn't get to go at the front

My dad parked next to me. He gave me a helmet and I sat behind him. He told me that I had to hold on really tight. He said I wasn't allowed to fall off. I couldn't take Mr. Ted because he couldn't hold on tight like I could. He had paws. I had fingers.

I hoped we drove passed people from my school. I wanted them to see. I was on my dad's bike. I wanted to show them. My dad was so big. He was like a Superman on a bike. I wanted to be like him when I growed up.

We didn't see any of my friends. But I kept looking just in case. My dad told me to leave the helmet with the bike. I wanted to take it with me. Then I was like a real biker with my helmet and everything. My dad didn't mind. He said as long as I didn't lose it. I would have to pay for it if I did. I didn't get any money. I didn't know how I would pay. I promised I wouldn't lose it.

The library was huge. Like for giants. In the front was a big floor. The picture was made from tiny square stones. There were five doors. I could see in all of them. They had all the books in the world.

Each door had a sign above it to say what kind of books. My dad took me through the one that said travel. Inside all the doors went to the same place. It was like magic. My dad took me through some books. The shelves were so high not even my dad could reach the top. He was big too. There was a ladder though. It said 'Do not use' I wondered how you got the books if you could not use the ladder.

At the back of the library there was another door. It was big and bright. It had a rainbow on the top. My dad told me that was where my books were. He took me in and we talked to the library lady. She asked my name and I told her. She asked how old I was. I said. Five. Then she gave me six cards. I could take six books from the library if I wanted to. Six whole books.

I had never got six whole new books before. My dad said he was going to look at his books. He said that I was to sit in the corner and read. He would come back soon for me. I wished Mr. Ted was there. I could have showed him all the books. He would like so many. It would be like getting presents. Just for us.

I sat on the squishy bag. I put on my dad's helmet. It made my face scrunchy. I didn't know when it was time to go. I read nearly all the book. I hadn't got time to get six books. I had been reading too much. About a boy that lived by the river. He was an orphan. I felt sad for him. But he had lots of fun all the time. Maybe that was what it was like when you had no mum and dad. I wondered if he got frightened at night time like I did. Maybe he was good and didn't get a bad man either.

My dad told me to get one book quickly. He said we would read it at bed time. He showed me a collection of books that you could buy. They weren't a lot of pennies. My dad said I could have one if I wanted. They were called Mr. Men. There were lots of them. On the back was a picture of all the different Mr. Men. I wondered if I could get them all and we could cross them off. I picked one called Mr. Bump. My dad bought it for me.

When we got home it was late because my dad had to keep going places to do things. It was dark when we got in the house. My mum said we had missed dinner so there wasn't any. It was okay. I didn't get many dinners. I sat in my spot by the fire and the chair. I showed Mr. Ted my books. I didn't say it out loud. He could read minds too. My mum didn't like it when I talked to Mr. Ted. She told me to stop being a baby. She didn't understand he was magic. "You'll get sent away if you carry on," she said. "To a place where they don't ever let you out." I didn't want to get sent away. But I wanted to talk to Mr. Ted.

When I got to go to bed my dad said he would read to me. He said we could read my Mr. Bump book. I didn't get to be frightened of the bad man because my dad came with me. He told me to get changed and get in bed. I did. He got in with me.

He let me lie on his arm again. He did the thing again. He put his hand in my pyjama bottoms. I moved his hand. I didn't want him to do that. He didn't tell me off. He just read. He did it again. I didn't tell him no. I rolled away. When I started to fall asleep because my dad was telling me about clumsy Mr. Bump he put his hand in my pants again. I didn't roll away. I just let him have his hand there.

He got my hand and pulled it behind me like last time on his private parts. I closed my eyes. I made it all dark. I didn't want my dad to do what the bad man did. I didn't like it. I pretended I was asleep. I let him keep my hand on his thing. I listened to him read.

## FOURTEEN

Little boy, little boy,
The bad mans in there,
Don't go, don't move,
He'll give you a scare.

When we waked up in the morning my mum said we were going to church. Her church. She wanted to take me there. Maybe they could help with the evil. I wondered how they would do it. My mum didn't give me medicine that day. She said it was okay. I didn't need it to go to church. "The church needs to see exactly what I have to deal with day to day," she said.

My dad didn't say anything. He was reading his paper. Drinking tea from his giant mug and smoking a cigarette. My dad didn't go to the church like my mum did. Only sometimes. When she shouted at him for it. He thought it was "a load of codswallop" but sometimes my mum got mad and said he didn't care. So he would go.

He wasn't coming with us though. He was going to look after my brother. He was going to drive us to the church and then he would take my brother to the beach while the church looked for my evilness. I wished I could go to the beach. I had only ever been with my Nan. She took me on a pier. I got to play on the machine thing. I put pennies in and tried to make other pennies fall out. Like a waterfall. I got so many pennies that it made my shorts want to fall down. My Nan laughed because I had to hold them up.

It was going to take me forever to spend all the pennies. My Nan gave me a chocolate box. It was made of tin. The lid creaked so I had to be quiet. I put my pennies in there. I also put my papers in there. Where me and Mr. Ted wrote our stories.

When breakfast was finished. We got into the car. We had to wear our Sunday bestest. "Don't want the neighbours to think we're a bunch of tramps," my mum said. So I had on pants and a shirt. She made me wear a stupid tie. I didn't like it. It was big and hanged down. She told me off for biting it.

It was a million miles away to the church. It was hot in the car. My mum wouldn't let me put the window down. She said it was too cold outside. My dad put his window down. He blew his smoke out of it. I tried to tell her he had one open. She told me to be quiet.

I wished I had Mr. Ted with me. He had to stay at home. My mum said I couldn't take him in case I lost him. I would never lose Mr. Ted. Not ever. But she still said no. She said I had to be good. I tried really hard. But my mouth just wanted to be bad. I felt bad inside. My badness. It made my mouth say things that got me in trouble. Maybe it was because I didn't get no medicine. Maybe the medicine just worked for one day. Like super powers. And then at night time when the clock made a noise it went away and I got bad again. She told me if I didn't stop it I was going to get a clip around the ear.

When we got to the church my mum made me stay with her. It wasn't really a church. It was pretend. The church that we went to at school was big. It had funny windows with lights. But it said church outside.

I wondered if they had a graveyard. Maybe they lived in this church. Did the dead get woken when they were noisy? I didn't want dead people in my garden.

A man answered the door. He hugged my mum. She smiled. He made her happy. He was old. He had funny white hair. He told us to come in. The lady that lived there. She asked if I wanted a drink. I didn't know if I was allowed to say yes. I looked at my mum and she nodded. So I said "yes please."

We went into some rooms. It was at the back of the house. There were big doors. The garden was like a giant's. It was so green. Like he had his own park all to himself.

The man sat down on the chair near me. He told me to sit on the sofa. I didn't get to sit on sofas before. I sat on the edge. I wished I had gone with my dad.

He asked me what happens when I feel bad. I didn't know what he wanted me to say. I shrugged my shoulders. He told me that my mum was poorly. He said that it was my job to be good. I shouldn't do bad things because it made her sad. He asked if I understood and I nodded.

I didn't try to be good all the time. Sometimes, I had thoughts that made me bad. I didn't know how to keep them away.

I told him that I got scared at night. I said that I got bad dreams about a bad man. He told me that I just needed to be good. He made me promise. I promised.

The man said his name was Brother Marcus. He was going to help me and my mum to make it all better. I sat on the sofa. Brother Marcus and my mum sat at the desk. They talked about boring things. Like my mum did with her friend at the shop. It made me bored.

The nice lady brought me a drink of orange. She asked if I wanted to come and see the fishes she had. They were in the next room. She asked if I liked them. We had fishes at school. They were boring and little. But I said yes.

I went with the lady. The tank was giant. She had giant fish too. She told me their names, but the words were too long and I couldn't remember them. The giant fish got to swim around a big rock. It looked like a sunken ship. I wished I got to be a fish then I could pretend to look for treasure. I could be a pirate. I was going to tell Mr. Ted we could write a story about being pirates.

When I turned around to look at the lady. The bad man was at the door. He had a mug. He was drinking and leaning. He smiled at me and said hello. I felt funny inside. I wanted to go to the bathroom.

I didn't say hello back to him. My neck wouldn't let any words come out.

I went back to the other room where my mum was and stood next to her. I stared at the door. The bad man was there. In the light time. I told him in my brain that I didn't be bad. I was sorry. I wanted to get invisible. My pants got wet.

Mr Ted.

Why did the bad man be there? I didn't be bad. Please tell him I wasn't. I didn't mean to get my pants wet. I just got scared in my tummy. It was on accident.

## FIFTEEN

Little boy, little boy,
Just stay still,
He won't get you today.
Don't think that he will.

I didn't know what to do. My mum got mad. She didn't shout at me. But I could see her mad eyes. She had a mad mouth too. I waited for her to shout at me. I watched the door to where the fishes lived. The bad man would come in a minute. No one was going to stop him. I was just too bad. Bad. Bad. All the time. I didn't know how to get good. I kept trying. All the time. I wanted to be good. The evil just found me. I started to cry. I didn't know what I was meant to do. I didn't know what to say.

I told my mum I was sorry. She shook her head at me. I was going to get in trouble when I got home. I wished I could run away. Then I could leave them alone. My mum wouldn't have to get mad at me all the time. Maybe I could go to my Gaga. I wished there was a way. I wondered how you got to heaven.

The nice lady got in the room. Brother Marcus told her what had happened. He told her about my badness. He didn't say it was the evil inside. But I knew it was. I always got bad. All the time. He asked her if there was something they could wrap around me. My mum told him it didn't matter. I could sit on a shopping bag.

"He does this all the time," she said. "Just the other day he decided to use the hallway as a bathroom, rather than walk up the stairs."

Brother Marcus looked at me. He did that tut tut thing that I got told off for. He asked me if there was a reason for it. I shook my head and said no. He told me to look at my mum. I did as he said. He told me to think about what it would be like to not have her. I couldn't imagine not having my mum. I didn't want to know what that was like.

I didn't saying anything. I didn't have any good words. I hugged my arms on me and cried. I didn't want my mum to go away. I didn't want to go away because I was too bad. I didn't want the bad man to come. I just wanted to go home to Mr. Ted. I was sorry for me. I was sorry that I was just bad all the time. I didn't mean it.

The bad man came into the room. He stood by Brother Marcus. He didn't speak to me. I hugged myself tighter because I wanted to squeeze myself away. I wished I could get invisible. I don't know why I did it. It was my badness I guessed. I walked out of the room. I could hear my mum saying my name. But my ears didn't want to listen. I didn't want to be there with the bad man. I didn't want him to get me while my mum was there.

I was the bad boy that wet my pants. I was a baby.

I got outside to the garden at the front. I went to stand at the pavement where the car was. My dad and my brother were still at the beach. My mum came outside. She didn't shout.

"Get back in there," she said. She made it like a whisper. But it was still a shout. She could shout and whisper at the same time. I shook my head.

"No," I said.

She grabbed my arm. Her fingers digged in. I wriggled to get her off me. But she was big and she could hold on tight. I shouted at her to let go. I pulled and made my legs flop so I tried to fall on the ground. She maked me stand up. She tried to make me go back to the house. But I didn't want to. I shouted at her. I told her I wanted to go home.

She let go of me. I fell on the ground. I sat against the car. Brother Marcus came to talk to me. I put my hands over my ears and closed my eyes. Maybe I could make him vanish. He kept talking. I didn't want to listen. My mum said she was going to find my dad.

I didn't know why covering my ears didn't work. When I closed my eyes it went dark. So I didn't know why I couldn't close my ears too. I pressed on them hard. I could hear a swish noise. But I could still hear the words Brother Marcus said. I tried to ignore him.

My mum came back with my dad. He didn't look mad. My brother ran ahead to me. I stood up. I didn't look at anyone. I knew I was in big trouble. I just wanted to go home.

My mum shouted all the way home. I squeezed myself together. I wanted to hide. I wanted Mr. Ted. I want to tell him I was bad and I was sorry. The bad man would get me anyway. I deserved it. I was always bad. It was no good. Maybe the bad man could take me away. He could tie my hands and feet like he did before. I didn't really know what he did. Mr. Ted told.

I digged my fingers into my sides. I tried to hurt my ribs. I squeezed too hard to make myself feel it everywhere. The bad man would come and he would make it hurt too. I could make it hurt better. I digged into the skin until it was under my nails.

My mum turned in her seat when she shouted; she looked at me and wagged her finger at me. "I wished I'd never had kids," she said. She used her bad words again. "It's your fault," she said to my dad. "You forced him here, this is what I get. I should never have got married. I never wanted kids."

I made her even not want my brother. My evilness did everything wrong. I was just too bad inside.

When we got home. My mum told me to get in the damn house. I walked too slowly. When they opened the door and I walked in my dad got mad. He smacked me at the back of my head. It made me fall over. I fell into the house. I cried loud at what he did. When I turned around he bent down and hit me across the face. He yelled at me for everything. He asked why I didn't behave all the time. All I had to do was behave for one god damn day. I couldn't do that.

He dragged me up the stairs. I didn't want to go up there. It was light time, but I was bad. The bad man would come for me. My dad dragged me to the bedroom. I tried to tell him I was sorry.

He pushed my hands away. He smacked me across the face again. Then he locked the door and went downstairs. I sat on my box. I hugged my knees. I didn't hug Mr. Ted. Only good boys got to hug Mr. Ted. Not me I was too bad for that. I pulled my hair hard. I didn't let go. Stupid boy. Bad. Bad. Bad.

Mr Ted.

Maybe you don't like me too.

## SIXTEEN

Little boy, little boy,
It's only this time,
Just do it and listen,
I promise you'll be fine.

I didn't move. I didn't dare. The bad man was coming that night. I was sure. I knew he would. I had been bad. The evil inside did it again. No one came. I stayed locked away. I didn't move. Not at all. Inside I needed to go to the bathroom. I didn't ask. I didn't shout. I knew the answer. I stayed alone. Alone in the dark with no one to come and get me. They all sat downstairs. Happy I wasn't there. Better without me. They didn't want me. I didn't want to hug myself anymore. I just cried. Alone.

My mouth was funny. I needed a drink. But I didn't get to ask. I knew they would say no. They put me here to keep me away. So they didn't have to see the badness inside. So they didn't have to see me.

It got dark. I made my ears listen. I had to listen for the bad man. I heard someone on the stairs. I listened to their walk. I knew it wasn't him. I told him lots and lots of times that I was sorry. I was bad. I knew I was bad. All inside. I wished I could go away and not come back. I wished there was somewhere I could hide that no one would ever find me. Maybe I could live there.

I wondered what it was like to live in a cave. When I saw it on the television. It looked fun. It got dark, but they had fire to keep it light. Maybe I could find a cave and hide there. Even Superman had a cave. He kept his things in there. No one ever went in. it was a secret place.

It was my dad's feet on the stairs. I curled myself on the box. I listened as he put my brother in bed and hugged and kissed him night-night. I hugged my legs. I listened to my dad. I didn't want him to go back down stairs. The bad man would come when he wasn't here. My dad wouldn't hear me. The bad man would make him not hear me shout like he did my mum. I tried to shout for her, but she never heard. It was like magic.

I wished I could ask my dad to stay. He opened the door and looked at me. I was sorry for being bad and for wetting my clothes.

He told me that I had to get in the bath. He said I could use my brother's water because I smelt from the day time and my badness.

I got in my brothers water. It was cold. My dad came in with me. He washed my hair and my body. He did the same thing with his hand on me. I didn't move his hand that time. I had been bad already. My dad talked to me about my books. He asked if I was sorry for what I had done. I said I was. He told me that I had to be good for my mum. "You should always do as she says," he said to me. I nodded.

I tried all the time. I just got bad. I couldn't help it. When the bath was done. My dad pulled the plug out. I stayed in the bath as the water went away. I was cold. I hugged myself up. But my teeth shaked again.

My dad gave me a towel. And then he gave me one of his t-shirts. It was too big for me. But I liked sleeping in it. It had scary pictures on the front with fire on. It was so big it was nearly touching my feet.

My dad told me to get in bed. I did. I got Mr. Ted too. I asked my dad if we were going to read. I wished he was going to say yes. I didn't want him to go away. The bad man would come. I had been bad. He had to come and tell me off.

My dad got into bed too. He let me lie on his arm. I got to rest my head on him. We were going to read Mr. Bump again. He said if I could be good we would go to the library again. He said we could get another Mr. Man book. I couldn't wait. It made me happy inside my tummy. I wanted to hug my dad and say thank you.

I followed the words with my eyes. My dad read. I liked how he made them sound. Mr. Ted lied between me and my dad. He was happy there. My dad's words made my eyes feel sleepy. I lied on him with my hand on his tummy. My dad got my hand and put it down into his pants.

# DEAR TEDDY

  I pretended to be asleep. I just listened while he read. He put my hand on his thing. I pretended to roll over while I was asleep. But my dad got my hand and stopped me. He put it back. He moved my hand like he did before. He had his hand on mine.

  I didn't do anything. I pretended. Mr. Ted pretended too. We were sleeping. When my hand got wet and sticky my dad stopped moving my hand. I pretended to roll away again. My dad didn't grab my hand that time.

  He finished reading Mr. Bump. I pretended to wake up. I asked my dad if I could use the bathroom. He said I could. I washed my hands hard. I washed each bit of them. Like my Nan told me to do if I had been playing in the mud or the sand. I didn't like my hands. They felt bad. Maybe they felt evil inside them. I tried to wash the evil away.

Mr Ted.

Please tell me what he did. It feels bad inside. My hands don't feel good. I feel the evil. It's here. I'm bad. Please take it away.

## SEVENTEEN

Little boy, little boy,
It's all a big trick,
Run and hide,
Come to me quick.

I didn't get to go to school again when the week started. My dad got me up. Me and Mr. Ted got breakfast. My mum gave me my medicine. But I got sick before she gave it to me. My neck hurt inside again. I got too hot. My mum told me that I needed to stay at home.

I hugged Mr. Ted. We sat by the fire next to the chair. I didn't talked to my brother. I wasn't allowed to. But my mum did let me make Lego houses. She said I could do it as long as I didn't make a mess. "And make sure I'm not finding those damn bricks all over the place, or I'll put them out with the rubbish," she said. So I looked after them.

I made a house and a police station. I made a fire station too. But the fire engine was lost. My brother had it in his room. I didn't want to go and get it. Maybe the bad man would be upstairs. I could pretend we had one. It didn't matter that it wasn't red. Or a fire engine. We just said it was.

When my Nan came to help my mum. She asked what we were doing. I told her I was making Lego for my brother. She asked why I wasn't going to school. I told her I wasn't well.

My Nan asked to look inside my mouth. I don't know what she was looking for. But she shouted my mum and told her to look too. My Nan said I should go and see the doctor.

My Nan called the doctors. She told them I was just five and that I was too hot. I didn't feel too hot. I felt too cold. I wanted some blankets. My Nan said I needed to get cool. But I was cold. I wished she believed me. It made my teeth shiver. I showed her, but she put a cloth on my head.

My dad had the car. We had to walk to the doctors. It was only a little bit near the house. My mum told me to sit on the floor in the waiting room. It was so boring. I had no toys. The books were boring too. They were full of boring things about houses and stuff. I wanted to go back home and play with the Lego.

My mum sat and talked to the lady next to her. I don't know what they talked about. Maybe it was old things. When the reception lady came out each time, I hoped that she was going to say my name. Then I could see the doctor. I wondered if he would give me a sticker. My brother got stickers when he went to the doctor. My mum said I couldn't get one.

Sometimes my brother got a lolly. It looked like a whistle, but it didn't make a very good noise. My mum still got mad about it. She would tell him to stop it with the damn noise. Then he would bite it.

When the lady did come and say it was my turn. I got afraid inside. Maybe he would see my badness. I followed my mum into his room. She sat on the chair and I stood next to her. She told the doctor about my neck hurting inside. He told me to open wide so he could see.

He put a stick in my mouth. It made my neck try and turn upside down like when I got sick in my tummy. I moved away. I didn't like it. I didn't want to get sick on the floor.

He asked me to lift my jumper up. I didn't want to. I wanted to go home. He made me afraid inside. I shook my head.

My mum told me to do as I was told to. But I didn't want to. My mouth was bad and said no. The doctor talked to me about school. I told him that I wanted to be a doctor when I was big. He asked if I wanted to put on his thing to listen inside.

He said it was called a stethoscope. I had seen my Gaga's. But I had not ever been allowed to touch it. I would break it.

The doctor put it in my ears. Then he told me to put it on my jumper. I did. I could hear the noise inside my tummy. He said if I put it inside my jumper I would be able to hear my heart. He put his hand inside my jumper and told me to listen. I could hear it. It was fast. Like trains. I wished Mr. Ted was with me then I could let him hear too. I told the doctor I could hear it. He asked if it sounded big and strong. I said yes. He asked if he could hear too.

I let him have a turn with the ear parts. He said that if I held my breath I could hear that too. So we did that and took turns.

He talked to my mum after. He said I could listen to all the different parts. I did. I tried to make my insides make noises.

I liked the doctor. He was nice. I wanted to be a doctor like him. I was going to tell Mr. Ted. Then we could be doctors too and we could write about it.

After when me and my mum walked home, she got me to the corner and made me stop. I didn't move. I was in trouble for saying no. She asked me why I had to be bad. "Why do you always have to show me up like that," she said.

I didn't know why. I was just frightened in my tummy. I told my mum I was sorry. I said that I knew the doctor was her friend and I wouldn't be bad again.

She asked me about the doctor being her friend. I said that he smiled at her. I thought that he liked her because she was a nice mum. She asked me if I really thought so. "If you're telling me lies," she said.

"Then you know I will know. And then you'll be in trouble."

I shook my head the hardest I could. I didn't tell lies. The doctor was nice. She asked me if he smiled a lot at her. I said he did. I said he must think she was the best mum in the world. I waited for my mum to shout at me. She didn't. We went home.

My Nan got me a stethoscope. It was red. There was a box to keep it in. And lots of others things that the doctor had. She asked if I had been good. My mum said I had, so my Nan said I could have it.

I put the doctor things on Mr. Ted. I told him he was now Dr. Ted. I couldn't hear anything in his tummy. Maybe he had too much fur.

When my Nan went home. My mum made dinner for me and my brother. She gave me the medicine the doctor had given. It was nice. I wanted some more. She let me sit at the table with my brother. Even Dr. Ted could sit with us.

When we had eaten she said we could play. I wanted to play like Superman . The medicine made me feel better. I put the Doctors clothes on Dr. Ted and my mum let me put a blanket on me like a cape. I didn't get told off when I standed on the chair and jumped off.

I wanted to be like Superman . I wondered if now that Mr. Ted was a doctor he could make me fly. I held his paw and we jumped off the chair. I just kept landing on the floor. I jumped my hardest. But it never worked. I didn't know why I couldn't fly like SSuperman .

When my mum had washed the dishes and smoked her cigarette. She said that it was time for my bath. My brother was in bed. My dad wasn't back from work. She told me to go upstairs and use the toilet. I got scared. She said she would come with me.

I went into the bathroom and my mum sat outside on the top of the stairs. I brushed my teeth my fastest and went to the toilet. I opened the door to tell my mum that I was ready for my bath. But she was gone. The bad man was there.

Mr Ted.

He's here. The bad man. He's going to get me. Please tell him I'm sorry. I didn't be bad. I just got scared. The doctor is nice. Please tell him. Don't hurt me.

## EIGHTEEN

Little boy, little boy,
Hold on tight,
You'll get through this, I promise,
Just don't fight.

He was there. He smiled at me. He was there and he smiled. My mum was gone. The bad man was there. I got frozen. I couldn't get my mouth to shout my mum. I didn't hear her leave. I didn't hear the bad man come. I couldn't see my mum. Maybe he had hurt her.

He smiled.

I tried to get back in the bathroom. I could close the door and open it again. He would be gone. My mum would be there. I moved. The bad man moved. Like he was copying. I jumped back into the bathroom. I tried to get the door closed. I screamed my loudest for my mum. The bad man was bigger. He pushed the door. It made me slide. I didn't have any powers to make the door keep closed. I tried to make my wellies stick to the floor. But it didn't work. The floor was slippery. I just slipped with the door when he pushed it. I shouted my loudest and my hardest for my mum. I wanted her to come and make him go away. I didn't want the bad man to get me. I had tried to be good. I hadn't been bad. Not bad so he had to come in the light time. I wished Mr. Ted could tell the bad man I was good.

The bad man got in the bathroom. I shouted for my mum. I shouted as loud as I could. The bad man didn't scare away. He turned me around and he bent my arm on my back. It hurt so bad. I thought it was going to break off. I couldn't get my arm away. I cried because he hurt me. His big hands squeezed my arm. I thought he was going to make it fall off like I did with toys sometimes.

I told the bad man I was sorry. I cried and promised I wouldn't be bad no more. I would crossed my heart. I would never be bad again. Even if the evil tried to make it. I wouldn't.

The bad man pulled my Superman cape. It strangled my neck. My neck hurt. I didn't get to shout because the cape was too hard on my neck. It made my neck feel like fire inside.

He pushed me on the bath. It digged into my tummy. He pulled my shorts off and my underpants. He squashed me down hard. I couldn't move. He took his own pants down. I didn't like his face. It was scratchy on mine. He told me that this is what I got for being a bad boy. He said bad words about what happens to bad boys. He was big and heavy. He squashed me down because he lied on my back. He digged his hands into my legs. Then he hurt me with his thing. It made me scream my hardest. It made me cry. The bad man hurt me more with his thing.

It hurted so bad inside. I screamed for Mr. Ted. I think my head popped. Because it went dark. Like a bang inside all my body. I think I exploded. Maybe into a million pieces. Like humpty dumpty. Maybe they could never put me back together again.

I thought he was going to hurt me forever. It was a long time. But the bad man let me go. I was too tired to move. I didn't know how to get up. He let me lie on the floor by the bath. He stood up and smoked a cigarette. He laughed at me. I didn't want to look at him. I wanted my mum. I wanted her to hug me like my Nan did if I fell over and got banged. I felt sick in my tummy.

I hugged myself on the floor. I didn't get to move. All my pieces were broken. They all hurt. I shaked. But I wasn't cold. My body just wanted to do the shiver thing again. I closed my eyes and went to sleep.

When I waked up again. I was in my mum and dad's bed. I had pyjamas on. My hair was wet. I didn't remember getting in the bath. The covers were tight. Not like when the bad man did it. Just tight like when my mum did it. I couldn't move. And I hurt. Mr. Ted was next to me.

I felt sick in my tummy. I started to cry because I didn't want to get sick in the bed. But I hurt to move. I didn't want to go to the bathroom in case the bad man was there still. I didn't know where my mum was. Maybe he had got her. The room was dark. The hallway was dark too. Maybe the bad man had got everyone.

I shouted. But not loud. I didn't want to make the bad man come. I heard the door downstairs. Then I heard my dad's feet. My dad came into the bedroom my dad asked me if I wanted to go downstairs. I nodded. I couldn't get up. I was too heavy.

My dad opened the covers. I hugged Mr. Ted and my dad picked us both up. He was big and strong. He carried me and Mr. Ted down stairs. The fire was on. My dad put me on a big cushion in front of it. He gave me a blanket and I made myself in a ball.

My mum made me some tea. She asked me if I felt better. She told me that I got sick in the bathroom and she put me to bed. I didn't tell her about the bad man. Maybe she didn't see him. If I told her he would know and he would come back. I drank my tea. It was hot and had lots of sugar in it. I liked my mum's tea the best. It was always so nice. My Nan and dad didn't put sugar in theirs. It didn't taste as good.

I tried to fall asleep. When my mum and dad watched the television I pretend I was asleep. I didn't want them to send me to bed. Maybe the bad man was still hiding up there.

When I needed to use the toilet I asked my mum. I used the outside one because I had got bad. But I liked the outside one better. There was no bad man out there. It was at the bottom of the garden. My mum didn't like to use it because of the spiders. But I didn't mind.

It hurt inside my body to walk. It hurt my legs too. I cried when I sat on the toilet. My tummy hurt inside. There was blood inside my clothes. I asked my mum. She came outside with me. I showed her. Maybe I was going to go to heaven with my Gaga. She said I wasn't. She said it was because I needed the toilet. She took me into the kitchen and gave me some more medicine. Not what she made. It was some from a box.

My mum took me in the house. She got a big bowl and filled it with water. She didn't use her cleaning powder. She used my brother's special bath stuff. She put it on the floor in front of the fire and told me to take my clothes off. My clothes had lots of blood in them. She said she would get me some more.

She told me to stand in the bowl. She used a cloth to make me clean again. I didn't like being cleaned by the fire. I stared at the television while she did it. I wanted to get dressed. She told me to turn around. But it hurt when I moved. She gave me medicine for that too. It just made me tired.

My mum helped me when I needed the toilet all the time. It made me cry. I didn't let my mum see me cry. She would think I was a baby. She would ask why I was crying. She waited outside in the garden. She didn't get mad when it took me too long. She didn't get mad when my pyjamas got a mess from the blood. Not like when I cut my knee.

At dark time when my mum and dad went to bed. My dad carried me and Mr. Ted to bed and I stayed there all night. When my mum was sleeping. I held her nighty so she couldn't leave. I didn't want her to get out of bed and leave me alone.

In the morning again my dad took me downstairs. I didn't want any breakfast. My dad asked me if I felt better. I didn't say anything. I didn't want to talk. He let me sleep on the cushion. My mum didn't give me my cure. She said I could have soup for my lunch. But I didn't want any. I didn't want anything.

I didn't eat. I didn't talk. I couldn't be bad. The evil wouldn't get me if I just lied there.


Mr Ted.

What did I do? He hurt me too bad. Maybe I just be too bad. It hurt and I cried. Why me? Why can't I just be good and it all go away?

# DEAR TEDDY

## NINETEEN

Little boy, little boy,
At school too,
Just come home,
I'll look after you.

When I got better again, I got to go to school. I had been so poorly and I had lied there by the fire all week. I did go to the library with my dad though. On Saturday. He let me buy another book. He said because I had been sick I could have two. I got Mr. Tickle and Mr. Green. We read my three books. Mr. Bump on the Friday night. Then Mr. Green on Saturday and Mr. Tickle on Sunday.

I didn't like touching my dad's thing. But I did like lying on him in bed. I liked the way he made the book sound. He could read better than me. He didn't have to stop. The bad man didn't come. I did what I got told to do. I was good.

When I went to the library with my dad. I changed my books too. The library lady asked if I had read them all. I told her I did. I liked reading. My mum showed me how to read. She said that it was good to be able to read things.

At school I could read bestest than anyone. My teacher let me read out loud sometimes. I got to read in the big class. Because I could read better than my class. I could write too. That's when I wrote my stories. I liked to make funny things happen in my stories like they did in books. I liked it in books when they made me laugh. Sometimes I got told off for it. My mum said I was being noisy.

In the big class. I didn't like one of the boys at school. He was new. He was big and tall. He was mean. He didn't like me either. He was strong and he pushed me over sometimes.

When we were all in the yard together he made me stand behind a wall. He told me that if I moved he was going to beat me up. He said if I moved he would get me in trouble. I didn't want to get in trouble because then the bad man would know and he would come and get me and hurt me again.

I did as Simon said. I stayed by the wall. When the bell went he told me not to move. I cried because I didn't know which was bad. I was going to be in trouble for not going back into school. I was going to be bad if I did go into school. I stayed in the corner and cried.

The lollypop lady found me. The nosey old bat lady. She asked what I was doing. I shrugged my shoulders and told her I didn't know. She took me into the office. I got in trouble off my teacher for hiding. She said she was going to tell my mum when school finished.

When school got finished my teacher told my mum. She didn't say anything. We walked home. My mum walked home with Simon's mum. They got to be friends. We walked behind them. Simon hit me in the arm. He kept hitting me. I told him to stop it, but he said no. So I hit him back as hard as I could. He cried. He ran to his mum and said I had hit him.

My mum and his mum stopped. My mum grabbed my arm and asked me what was wrong with me. The teacher had told her about me not going back in school. And then I hit Simon. She asked why I was bad all the time. I didn't know why I got to be bad. It just happened.

She told Simon's mum she was sorry. She grabbed my neck at the back. Her nails were big. They digged into my neck. I tried to wriggle and get them off. But she just did it harder. She dragged me all the way home again.

She told me that I was spoilt. My Nan was there. My mum said I had been bad. My Nan looked sad at me. When she had to go home she told me I should be good for my mum. She said my mum was tired. I told my Nan I would try.

When my Nan went home I told my mum I was sorry. My mum said I was an evil child. She hated that she got made to have me. She was sorry she had ever had me. I was sorry too.

My mum told me to get out of her sight. She opened the back door and told me to go out. She said she had, had enough. She didn't want me in the house. She didn't want to look at me. "You better get yourself back here when your father gets home," she said. "Or there will be trouble."

I didn't go very far. I played in the alley behind the house. I found a tennis ball. All the fur had gone off it. But it still bounced. I played with it against the wall. There was a boy and a girl. They came and played in the alley. The boy asked if I wanted to play catch. I said yes. So we did. We stood in a triangle and threw the ball.

They told me they were called Phillip and Anne. They were brother and sister. Anne was one year older than me. They lived in the house at the end of the alley. It was big and clean. It looked shiny.

When my dad came home. I heard his motorbike. I told Anne and Phillip that my dad had a big bike. When he came in the alley I showed them. My dad didn't say hello to me though. Maybe he knew about my badness already. I didn't tell Anne and Phillip about my badness. I wanted them to be my friend.

I told them I had to go in for dinner. They asked if I could play out after. I said I couldn't that my mum would want me in the house. Phillip said we could play tomorrow. I felt excited inside.

My mum was waiting by the back door. She was smoking her cigarette. My dad was there. She told me to get into the damn house. I knew she was going to hit me when I walked passed her. I didn't move.


Mr Ted.

Why does no one like me? Maybe I am just too bad. I don't mean to be. I want to be better. But I can't. No one likes me. Not ever.

## TWENTY

Little boy, little boy,
You're not all bad,
Just a little boy, a child
They like to be mad.

The house was scary like in my books. Where the monsters hid. They waited to get me and then they eated me all up. I didn't want to go in the scary house. My mum yelled at me. "Get in this damn house now," she said. She used bad words. She called me bad names. It maked me shake when she said them.

Such a bad boy all the time. I told myself in my brain. I was just bad. Bad and bad. It didn't matter. I could not be good. I put my hand in my pocket on my shorts. I could feel my leg. I digged my nails in and digged hard so it hurt. I didn't cry. Bad boys didn't get to cry. You can only cry when it is on accident. But my badness was there.

I couldn't get the badness away. It made me shake my head. I didn't want to go in the house. My tummy was sick inside. I got frightened because the bad man was going to come when it got to dark time. I made my fingers hurt my leg more. I told the bad man in my brain that I was doing it. He didn't have to hurt me bad like before. I did it for him. I wanted to make a hole in my leg. So it got too sore.

I told my mum I thought she was going to hit me when I got into the house. I said I didn't want to get hit. She got happy. She smiled. She said she wasn't going to hit me. But I was still scared she would. I said to her lots of times that if I went inside she was going to hit me. She said she wasn't. She promised. She said she just got mad but it was gone now.

My dad was drinking his tea. I could see him through the window. He didn't look mad. I told my mum ok. I went to the house. I squashed myself to the door and watched her hand so she didn't hit me.

She didn't. Like she promised. She closed the kitchen door and told me to go to the backroom and sit and be quiet.

My dad made me jump. He jumped so fast out of his chair. It crashed on the floor. I didn't get to go anywhere. He got me and he hit me on the face. My mum was shouting at him. She told him how bad I was. She shouted that she had to put up with this all day long.

My dad asked me if I was listening. He asked if I knew why my mum was upset. He said that I didn't get to go to the library on the weekend because I was so bad. He hit my legs. I had shorts on. His hand was hot. It made my skin like fire when he hit it. It was loud and hard. I tried to move my leg away. He did it again and again.

My brother cried. My mum got mad at that. She told me look what I made them do. Look how I made everyone in the house upset. Now I had upset my brother too. I didn't deserve the good things I had. She told me I was ungrateful.

My dad had my arm in his hand. I tried to go onto the floor. But he made me stand up. It hurt to stand. My body wanted to lie on the floor. I didn't want to get wet in my pants. But I could feel it there.

I told him to stop. I told him that I was sorry. I tried to hug myself but he didn't let me. My mum was still shouting. She didn't believe that I was sorry. She told me that she wished I wasn't there. She said that my dad made her have me and now she had to put up with me.

She got on her knees in front of me. She shouted at my face. She shouted so bad she spitted on me. Her eyes were mad. I cried because I wanted her to not shout at me. I didn't like when she was mad. I didn't like it when she hated me so much.

She got mad because I cried. She told me to go out into the hallway. I told her I was sorry. I didn't want to go out there. She said she didn't care. She got my arm off my dad and dragged me into the hallway.

She made me stand in the corner. She told me I wasn't allowed to move. I had to stand by the corner and think of how bad I was. Then she went back into the back room. She told my dad he had to deal with me because she had, had enough of it all.

My dad didn't shout at me. He held my arm and then he smacked my legs the hardest. He looked at me and made me look at him. "Don't you dare make a sound with your crying," he said. Then he made me turn around and told me not to move. He went into the back room.

I knew the bad man was upstairs. I could feel it. I think he was watching me. I kept looking. I know I wasn't supposed to move, but I did. It was on accident. My head turned because I thought he was there. I knew he was going to get me. It made my tummy not want to breathe.

When it started to be dark I watched the shadows and the glass in the door. I could see if he tried to sneaked up on me. My dad put my brother to bed before he went out on his motorbike. Then he told me to get upstairs. My legs didn't want to move.

He told me to go to the bathroom. Use the toilet and brush my teeth. I did what he said. I kept listening for the bad man's feet. I didn't want him to be there when I opened the door again. I couldn't brush my teeth because I was frightened inside. I tried. But it made me cry. I shaked while I did it. I didn't shut the bathroom door properly. I had to watch the shadows so he couldn't get me again. When I had to spit I did it fast and checked the door again. He was going to come in. It was like pretend. My skin pretended he was there. It made the scratches feel.

The dark time made me see things. Like pretend in my brain. I kept seeing the bad man. I knew he was smiling. He kept smiling at me and then he got me. I didn't know how to make the pictures go away. They made me more scared.

When I got finished I looked out in the hall slowly. I didn't want him to jump out at me. I didn't want him to get me again. But there was no one there. My dad had said to go to the bedroom when I was done. But I was too scared. I didn't go back downstairs. But I didn't go to the bedroom. I standed still. I wished Mr. Ted was with me. He could tell the bad man to go away.

I didn't know that my mum was in the bedroom. She came out. She got mad because I standed there and did nothing. She told me to get into the bedroom like I was told. The bad man wasn't there. My mum had just been in there. So I did as she told me to. She told me to get in bed.

I got in bed. I held Mr. Ted and lied very still. My mum turned the lamp off and went away.

The bad man came. But I fell asleep.

Mr Ted.

I'm so scared. I wish I didn't get to be. But I know the bad man keeps coming. I made my Daddy mad. He doesn't like me.

## TWENTY ONE

Little boy, little boy,
It's just a day out
Keep quiet, be brave,
No need to scream or shout.

I liked Phillip and Anna. They got to be my friends. They didn't go to the school I went to. They went to a special one because they were Catholics. When I told my mum about them she said that Catholics brainwashed you. They made you do things you didn't want to. I didn't think Phillip and Anne were like that. They were nice. They shared their sweets with me and we got to play games.

If I took my medicine and got to be good. My mum let me play out. I had to be back at six. "Not a minute later," she said. There would be trouble. I didn't get to be late. My Nan had got me a watch. At nearly six it played "Yankee Doodle," and I had to go home again.

Sometimes, I just pressed it so it played the song. When I played with Phillip and Anne we got to play pretend. I made stories up and we pretended to be them. At night when I got to bed. I would tell Mr. Ted about it. He thought it was good. Me and Mr. Ted would think of more games for me to play.

In the morning my mum would give me my medicine. If I got it fast I could go out the alley and walk to school. My mum said I could walk by myself. I had to go right to school. Phillip and Anne walked to school in the alley too.

I didn't tell them about the sick in my tummy. But I did like to walk with them. Sometimes Phillip would have fruit. He didn't like it. He would give it to me. I liked it best when he had oranges chopped in paper. I keeped it in my pocket and ate it on the break time.

When I got to finish school my mum would let me play out. But I had to get changed first. She made me fold my clothes so I didn't get my uniform creased. If it didn't get folded properly. She maked me fold it again until it was right. I didn't know why. I asked Mr.

Ted. My mum always folded it after. I wondered why she didn't fold it first.

My mum had a friend coming from the church. She told me that I couldn't see Phillip and Anne. I had to go out with her. I got excited because I didn't go out with my mum before. Except to the church. Her friend had a big white car. It was big and new. Not like ours. The one we had was old and had patches on it where my dad got to fix it.

My mum said we were going to go for a drive. My brother got to stay with my Nan because he was sleeping. When I got in the car with my mum it was the bad man. He was driving. He had a flat hat on. He said hello and said my name. I didn't get to talk to him. He made me scared inside. I wanted to go back to play with Phillip and Anne.

When he drove he looked at me in the mirror. My eyes kept looking at him too. I didn't like it when he saw. He smiled at me and I tried to make myself invisible. My mum said that we were going to go to the park. She said that the bad man liked to take pictures and he was going to take some of my mum.

She had on a blue dress. I had not seen it before. My mum always wore pants. She looked very pretty. Maybe my dad thought she was pretty too. She had her hair down and curly. She got to be smiling.

We got to a big park. It was next to the zoo. I got to the zoo once with school. I liked it in there. We watched a monkey eat his own snot. The girls thought it was yucky.

I didn't walk next to the bad man. I let my mum walk. She liked him and they held hands. He didn't be bad to me. He told me about things. He showed me his camera. I tried to hide behind my mum. But she told me not to be rude. I told the bad man it was very nice.

My mum sat on a tree. It had got fallen over with the winter. It fell over the water. My mum sat on it and the bad man took pictures of her. He kept making her move her hair and take her dress off her shoulder. It was boring. I asked if I could play. My mum said yes.

I got to play in the forest. I got to play pretend. I was sad that I had left Mr. Ted at home. Maybe we could go here with Phillip and Anne. We could play forest games. Maybe there were witches hiding that would eat us all up. I got to make the stories in my brain. I would tell Mr. Ted about them when I got home and then we could write then and make pictures. Mr. Ted liked it when we made pictures. But we didn't be allowed to draw about the bad man. If we did that he would come and get us.

I didn't get to say what the bad man did. I knew he would know. He said so. If I told anyone he would get me. No one would come and help like they didn't all the time. He wouldn't ever stop. So I didn't say. I didn't even say to the bad man. Bad words out loud.

He took lots of pictures of my mum. He took some the same as the ones my dad had in his comics. My mum looked funny with her dress down like that. I played my game. I didn't look at my mum. I didn't look at the bad man.

When they had finished taking pictures. We went back in the car. My mum gave me a drink and a sandwich. We were driving. I was tired. The car made me tired. I lied on the floor behind my mum's chair and closed my eyes.

I fell asleep. I must have gone far into sleep land. I didn't remember my mum taking me in the bad man's house. I didn't remember anything. It was dark time. I didn't like being near the bad man at dark time. I didn't know whose house we were in. My eyes looked funny. Like fairies in the air. I tried to grab them but there was nothing there.

My mum came into the room. I hid between the sofa and the chair. I felt silly trying to catch things only I could see. Maybe my eyes were magic. I asked my mum if I could get dressed. I didn't get any clothes on. I didn't remember taking them off. I didn't know what happened. Maybe I just fell asleep like always.

Mr Ted.

I keep falling asleep. Bad things happen. I get sore all the time. But I don't know why. My mum says it's a demon. Because I got evil. Please make me be good.

## TWENTY TWO

Little boy, little boy,
The bad man is real,
You're not dreaming I promise,
You know how you feel.

I didn't tell my dad about the bad man or the pictures. I knew if I did the bad man would come. It wasn't good to talk about him. Not ever. That made bad things happen. I didn't talk to the bad man anyway.

I told Mr. Ted about it though. I told him about the pictures and the forest. Maybe it would be a good place for us to play. We could take Phillip and Anne.

I hadn't seen the bad man for two days. I had been good. He hadn't needed to come. My mum had let me lie by the fire. I was cold inside again. I lied with Mr. Ted and we read my library book.

My mum was in the kitchen cooking. Someone knocked on the front door. She went to answer it. It was the bad man. She let him come in. I pretended to be sleeping. But he sat with me. He didn't be mad at me though. I had not been bad.

He sat on the floor next to me. He picked up my book and asked me what it was about. I didn't want to talk to him. I shrugged my shoulders. He opened the book and looked at it.

"Maybe you are not smart enough to read this," he said.

I didn't say anything. I could read it. I had read it with Mr. Ted. But I didn't want to talk to the bad man. He made me feel funny inside. The bad man got under my blankets with me. He showed me the book and asked me to read some words, but I didn't. I didn't want him to think I couldn't read if I said them wrong.

Sometimes when me or Mr. Ted didn't know words. We made them up from the letters. The teacher at school said that's what I was supposed to do. She showed me how to cover letters with my fingers. I had shown Mr. Ted. I didn't want to show the bad man.

The bad man told my mum that he thought there was something wrong with me. He thought I should see a special doctor to get fixed before it was too late. They talked about my evilness. My mum told him about how I heard the devil and he made me do bad things. The bad man said he knew about this.

They talked about my medicine.

The bad man had to go because my mum had to go to the doctors. She was taking me with her. But it wasn't for my badness. It was for my mum. But she wasn't sick. She just felt sad. Maybe she felt sad because I didn't be good. My mum said it was the same sick that made my big brother go away.

At the doctors I sat on the floor and read my book. My mum sat quiet. She looked sad. I asked her if she was okay. She said she was. When it was our turn to go to the doctor my mum told me to get up. She said I had to sit quiet while she talked to the doctor. I didn't know what they talked about. It was boring grown up things.

He gave mum some medicine. He asked me about school and about if I still was going to be a doctor. I said yes and I told him about the stethoscope my Nan had bought me. He said I should look after it.

There was a skeleton picture on the door. When I was looking at it. He asked me if I liked to know the names of the bones. I nodded and said yes. He told me lots of things. There was two hundred and six bones in our bodies. I wondered if when I got home me and Mr. Ted could count them all. When I looked at the picture it didn't look like that many bones. Maybe some were hiding.

The doctor gave me a sticker for being brave even though I hadn't been. It had been my mum that got brave not me. I just had a cold inside.

We walked home again. We was going to get my brother. But my mum got to the big road and she stopped. I asked her what was wrong because she didn't get to cross it when the man was green. She didn't talk to me.

I tapped my mum on the leg. She got my shoulder and digged her fingers in. She cried. "I want to go home," she said.

I said we could go home if she wanted. She told me that she was too scared. She cried and hugged herself. She was sounding like she had been running.

I told my mum she could hold my hand. She didn't want to. She said that she couldn't put her arms down. She was hugging herself. I said she was okay and it would be okay. We could get home very fast.

I told her we could go back to the doctors and maybe he could help her. She said no. She said he would think she was mad. I told her I didn't think so. He liked being her friend.

"Do you really think so?" she asked. I said yes. He was always nice to her. She said maybe he liked her like boys like girls sometimes. I said yes.

I told my mum if she held my hand we could walk home slowly. I promised I would show her how to get home. Me and Mr. Ted had learnt the way when we walked with my Nan. My Nan said it was good to know so we didn't ever get lost. I always had to cross at the green man or the zebra crossing. But my Nan told me to always wait till the cars have stopped. "You never know what these idiots are like," she said. Because idiots didn't stop cars.

I had seen it was true once. I had been shopping with my Nan and Mr. Ted. We had gone to get some things to make pancakes. The boy from around the corner was running. He run all the way to the zebra crossing.

He ran on the crossing. But the idiot in the car didn't stop. He bashed him with the car and the boy rolled up the car and then onto the ground again. My Nan went to him. But the boy got up and ran home. He had something wrong with his brain so he didn't feel anything.

Mr Ted.

My mum got scared today. I don't know why. I helped her, but it didn't be good. I don't know what I did.

## TWENTY THREE

Little boy, little boy,
Your mum is sick,
It's just your Dad
It isn't a trick.

I got my mum home. Nice and safe. We crossed all the roads. I talked to her about the doctor. She liked talking about him. It made her not scared. Like my Nan did with me when I got frightened. She would talk to me about things I did at school and then I didn't be frightened any more.

My mum went to the kitchen. I stayed in the back room. I watched her. She smoked her cigarette by the back door. She still looked sad. I didn't be allowed to go into the kitchen. But I did go. I asked my mum if I could use the toilet. I only got to use the outside one. She said yes and let me out.

When I was done I came back to my mum. I asked her if she was okay. She said she was and told me to get in the house and not to talk about silly things. I said I wouldn't.

I sat down by the fire and the chair with my book and Mr. Ted. My mum came in the back room when she got finished smoking. She asked me if I thought her things were silly. I said no. Sometimes I got scared.

She yelled at me. Using her bad words. She said that she wasn't five and what did I know. I told my mum I was sorry. I was just trying to help.

"Well you can keep your help to yourself next time," she shouted at me.

I looked at my book. I didn't read it. But I stared at the words and wished I could be in the story. Maybe then I didn't make my mum mad. I was sorry she got mad about it.

I didn't answer. That made her mad too. She told me I was being rude. "Because of you I'm going to have to call your Nan and ask her to come around here," she said. She told me to go to the bedroom. Because of my badness she didn't get to go for my brother. She got stuck in the house looking after me and dealing with my crap. But she said a bad word.

I didn't want to go upstairs. Maybe the bad man was here still. He might have come while we were out. I didn't remember seeing his car. But maybe he was there. I asked my mum if I could stay downstairs. I told her I was sorry. She said no. She said my Nan would be around at the house and she didn't want me there being bad so I had to go to my room. "And don't even think of coming downstairs," she said. "You know what all that crap causes when you do."

I knew what she meant. If I got to come downstairs, then the bad man had to be really bad with me. If my evilness got too much and just made me bad all the time.

I got Mr. Ted and went into the hallway. I was too afraid to go upstairs. Maybe Mr. Ted could talk to me about other things like I did with my mum. We walked up the stairs slowly. I had to be able to hear for the bad mans feet. I think my heart wanted to jump out. It banged so loud that maybe my mum could hear it.

# DEAR TEDDY

I didn't go to bed. I sat on the box and opened the window. I could smell the sunshine. It smelt nice. When I saw my Nan coming down the road I hid. I didn't want her to see that I was bad again. She would look at me and be sad about it. I didn't like her to know I was so bad.

I never did anything right. I wished I knew how to. Then maybe my mum would like me like she did my brother. I didn't know how to be better. I didn't want my Nan to know. She liked me. I didn't want her to see the bad things and decide I was bad too.

I hugged Mr. Ted. I told him about my mum. She had been frightened. I thought I got to help her. But I just made her mad all the time. Maybe one day we could leave. Then she could be happy we weren't around. She wouldn't have to put up with the "damn evil kid she got lumbered with," she would say. It made me sad when she said those words.

I didn't remember being asleep. When I opened my eyes I shouted. I forgot where I was. It was dark time. It wasn't the bad man there. It was my dad.

He was mad. I was sorry. Always sorry. I wished he knew.

"Why is your mother upset?" he asked me. I didn't know. I didn't know why she was mad at me. I shrugged my shoulders.

"I want an answer."

I didn't have answers. I didn't think Mr. Ted had answers either. He didn't know. He didn't see. I was just bad.

My dad told me to stand up. He took Mr. Ted and chucked him over the room. I tried to go to Mr. Ted. I didn't want him to be broken. My dad stopped me. He had big strong hands. They squished on my belly to stop me.

"I'm sorry," I said.

He told me that sorry wasn't good enough. He said if I was sorry I wouldn't be bad to start. He asked me why I always made her upset. He said she was crying because I made her cry. He shouted bad words at me and told me he had made her feel good and then I made it bad.

# DEAR TEDDY

He pulled me around with my arm. I screamed because it hurt. I thought he was going to make my arm come off. He pulled my pants down and smacked my legs and bottom. He did it lots of times until I screamed.

He swung me with my arm and let go. I fell to the wall. He knelt down with me. I thought he was going to smack me again. He didn't. He got mad in my face. He told me that in future I should keep my thoughts to myself. He got his hand and squashed my chin in it.

I didn't get up when he left the room. I could see Mr. Ted at the other side. He lied on the floor just like me. I hugged my arms. I got my fingers and digged them into my arms. Stupid boy. Stupid and bad and horrible.

I made my arms hurt because I was so bad. I put my fingers in my hair. I pulled hard because of the badness. I made it hurt lots and lots until I cried.

Mt Ted.

You should leave too. I'm too bad. I don't deserve you.

## TWENTY FOUR

Little boy, little boy,
It's just a treat,
At least she gave you
Something to eat.

When it got to Friday. My mum didn't say anything about the bad thing I did. I didn't want to asked in case it made her mad again. It was night time and my mum said that my dad wasn't coming home that night. He was doing something like school. I didn't know what it was. She said I could walk with her to the shop. She needed to buy cigarettes.

It was a walk along the road. Just past Phillip and Anne's. I didn't get to play with them yet because my mum said I had to stay inside. We went to the shop. I didn't look at the sweets and crisps. They made my tummy hungry. I didn't get to eat at home that week because of my badness. My mum said she forgot. Except when I got sent to the bedroom. Then I just didn't be good enough to get the food.

My mum asked me what I wanted. I didn't know what she meant. She asked again. "What do you want?" I looked at all the things in the shop. I only ever got to pick these things with my Nan. But I always got scared to pick. I didn't want to get greedy and then my Nan changed her mind and be mad at me. It made me feel funny when my mum asked. I didn't know what the right answer was.

She told me to pick one drink and one sweet. I did. I chose a bottle of coke and a bag of mixed sweets. I gave them to my mum and she paid the shop lady for me. I carried them all the way home. Maybe I had been good that my mum got me these things. I couldn't wait to show Mr. Ted. I would share them with him. Like a special surprise.

I told my mum about the coke. Because my Nan bought it. It made bubbles in my nose. My mum didn't say anything, but she didn't get mad and shout at me. My mouth just wanted to talk a lot.

At home. I got Mr. Ted. We sat by the fire and ate the sweets and drank the coke. I told him all about it and we read my book. My mum said she was going in the garden for a cigarette. I saw her through the window. I wanted to tell her thanks for what she had got me. I had never got things from her before.

When my mum had finished she came in the house and in the back room. She was mad. She had her angry eyes. I felt like I had been bad. Maybe my evilness got out. I looked at my book and not my mum. I didn't want to make her mad so she would send me upstairs.

She came in the back room. She shouted at me and told me that I did not say thank you for the things she had bought. I thought I did. I remembered saying it at the shop. Maybe my mum didn't hear me. I told her thank you again. I said it in a whisper. I thought she wanted to shout at me some more.

My mum came to me. She was mad. She snatched my coke bottle and threw it across the room. It smashed on the wall and made a pool on the floor. She told me that I didn't deserve nice things. That I always thought I was better than everyone in the house. But I didn't. I wasn't better. I told her that. I was the bad one. She didn't want to listen. She yelled bad names at me.

I wished I could give my mum my things back then she didn't be mad. I had my last sweet in my mouth. I tried to not cry. My eyes wanted to do it. The tears went down my face and into my mouth. They made my sweet taste like crying. I didn't want to sniff then my mum would know I was crying. I kept my book up so she didn't get to see. She would tell me I was stupid for crying. But I didn't get to stop it. It just happened.

I wished I could make my mum not be mad at me. Then she wouldn't shout. I wished I could give her back the things. I didn't know what I had done. Maybe I could be sorry if she told me, but she didn't.

She told me to put my book down and stop being so rude. She told me I was like my dad. That he did that. He just read his books and didn't listen. I swallowed my sweet. My mum took my book and told me to get upstairs to the room.

I did as she said. She came up too. She was shouting at me still. She kept telling me how bad I was. She told me to get changed and get into bed. I did that.

When I got in bed I hugged Mr. Ted under the covers so she didn't get to see. She told me that she wished she didn't get kids.

When she went downstairs. I listened to her feet go away. I closed my eyes and told Mr. Ted I was sorry.

The bad man came. I just fell asleep and he got there. My mum was in the bed too. Maybe it was lots of dark time. His hand slammed the bed next to my head. He made me jumped and frightened me. I moved back to my mum. She didn't wake up. Maybe he had made her fall asleep too.

He pulled the covers off me. I tried to keep them on, but he was big and strong and I couldn't do it. He pulled my clothes too. He digged his hand into my private areas. I cried because he used his nails and they made my skin bleed. I couldn't move away because he didn't let go.

He squished me down on the bed. It went dark. Maybe I went to sleep again.

Mr Ted.

My Mummy. She taked me out tonight. We got lots of things. But then she got mad at me and I don't know why. Did I be bad?

## TWENTY FIVE

Little boy, little boy,
Sing the song,
About Christmas and angels,
Your mother is wrong.

At school it got to be Christmas time. I liked that time. We did lots of things in the class. I liked when we made things that went into the big hall for everyone to see. The class was going to make a show of how baby Jesus came alive and how it was sad for his mummy and daddy because they didn't get a house and it was cold.

Maybe they didn't know it was Christmas time. I liked when we got to sing the songs. It just be practise. But I liked the way they made me feel inside. It was like singing in stories that I got to see on the television. But I felt sad about them being all alone at night.

I got to be an angel because I got blonde hair. I didn't like being an angel. I had to do dancing. It hurt sometimes when I got to dance. We did the show on the afternoon before the Christmas holiday. I had to get changed. I got on a big white t-shirt and my black pumps. It hurt to get changed because my back was sore.

I got bad the day before when my mum didn't get enough money for me to have some dinner. She had got my brother some chicken from the Kentucky fried chicken shop. It smelled nice and my brother had given me some. I ate it. I knew I wasn't allowed to. But I did and I got bad for it. My mum told me that it was stealing.

She had given me medicine from the morning time. She smacked my back hard and told me that I wasn't to have that chicken. It wasn't for me. She smacked my back until I got the sick in my tummy and then into the bin. But I got the sick wrong. I got sick too much. It came out too fast. Like my mouth went bang and everything came out. Some even came out of my nose. It made my eyes cry again.

She got mad because I got it on myself and she had to bathe me. She was going out with the bad man and I wasted her time like I always did.

It made it hard to get dressed at the school for being an angel. When I lifted my arms up I didn't want to cry and make my teacher mad. But my teacher got mad anyway. She asked me why I was taking so long. I said I didn't know. She told me to stop day dreaming.

We had to do it one time before all the mums and dads came to see. I tried my hardest. But it hurt too much to dance fast like everyone else. I really wanted to though. Maybe my mum or dad would come and see me. My Nan was going to come. I wanted to show her how good I got at school.

My teacher said that I could sit and watch if I didn't want to do it. I did. I told her I did and I was sorry. She made me go to the back because I was being bad and didn't get to be good like everyone else.

When it was time for us to show the mums and dads, we had to sit on the floor. It was hard and cold. It made me hurt because I got bad at home and the bad man had got me. I didn't be able to sit with my legs crossed. I sat so that I was on my legs. It made them feel funny. Like invisible again. The girl behind me said I was in the way. I didn't move though.

If I leaned my hands on my knees I could make my back not sore. But my tummy was sick inside because it was excited.

It got dark a little. It was all quiet. My Nan came. I saw her but I didn't look at her. I felt silly for smiling that she was there. I didn't want her to watch me in case it was wrong and she thought I was bad at it. I wanted my Nan to be there, but I didn't want her to see. I felt shy inside. I was glad when we got to sit down again.

We all did the show and sang the songs. Even the mums and dads sang the songs. I liked them. I wished I got to sing them lots of times. I liked Christmas.

After when we were all done. Santa came. He sat down and did his ho ho ho. Mrs. Boyle the headmistress stood up and got us all to clap hands because Santa was there. He had lots of cards. Ones that we all put in the letter box to our friends.

I didn't send any though. I tried. I wrote them all out. My Nan had bought them for me. But then I got writing them I didn't think anyone would want cards from me because I was so bad. I didn't put my name in them. I just told them Merry Christmas. When Santa gave all the things out I got lots and lots of cards. It made me smile in my tummy. I didn't know anyone liked me. I got lots of them.

When I walked home with my Nan. I read them all to her. I told her who everyone was. But I don't think she could remember them. I told Mr. Ted about the cards too. I felt sad because I didn't put my name in the cards I gave to Santa. Maybe they would think I didn't like them. I hoped they didn't get sad about it.

At home my mum said I could put the cards on string. I put them near the table where we ate dinner. There were so many I had to make them go over each other. I got more than anyone in the house.

My mum didn't be mad at me anymore. She said I could go and play out with Phillip and Anne. I had to be back at six. Then I got to go to bed and my dad read my Mr. Man book to me. The bad man didn't come when my dad read to me. Maybe what I did with my dad meant I got to be good.

Mr Ted.

It's nearly Christmas time. I have been good. I even was good for my Daddy. Maybe he lets me see Santa.

## TWENTY SIX

Little boy, little boy,
Write your letter,
Don't ask for things,
Just make it better.

I liked Christmas. It got me excited in my tummy. I liked Christmas Eve. My dad would show me what to leave out. We always left a mince pie and some wine and carrots for the reindeer. My brother got to put the things out. I helped him and told him about Santa. My mum didn't like me talking too much to my brother though. In case I made him bad like me. I didn't really get to talk to him at all. I didn't want him to get evil too.

We left the things out and then we got to have a bath. My brother went first and then I used his water. My mum didn't like me to go first because I got the water all dirty. I didn't like being second. The water always got cold.

I had written my letter to Santa. Mr. Ted had helped me. We asked him for a train set. I liked trains. I liked all the little towns. Me and Mr. Ted could make stories with them as we played. I wanted a bike too and a go-kart. Then I could play with Phillip and Anne when they went around on things like that. They let me have a turn on their things sometimes. I liked them very much.

When I went to bed my dad came too. He got a book. We had lots of them now. They didn't have Christmas Mr. Men books. I didn't mind though. We could pretend that they got Christmas. But my dad got me another book. It was one about the night before Christmas. I liked how he read it. It was like a rhyme.

I went to sleep with my dad there. The bad man wouldn't come with my dad in the room. He didn't ever.

On Christmas morning, I woke before my mum and dad. I didn't be allowed to wake them up. I lied there with Mr. Ted. It was dark time still. I wished it would be light soon then we could see if Santa had been. I didn't hear him come. I wanted to try. But my

Nan told me that if you catch Santa he gets frightened and his reindeer might run away. But maybe I could see him in the sky when he flied passed.

I asked my Nan how he got to come in our house. We didn't have a fire for him to get down like I had seen. It had a different one that got turned on with a switch. He didn't get to go down there. My Nan said he was magic. He would be able to get there.

I hoped Santa didn't get stuck down the chimney. Or begin to shout. I liked that song. "You boys and girls won't get any toys until you pull me out. Achoo, achoo, achoo," he said at the end. I liked that part the best. We got to do it at school. I always wanted to sing it again.

I waited till nearly light time. My brother woke up and he came into the bedroom. He climbed into the bed and my mum told me to get out and go to the toilet before we got to see Santa. I didn't want to go to the toilet. It got to be all the way outside. I didn't get to use the one in the house.

My dad got out of bed. He said he wanted a cigarette and tea before we saw the tree. I got downstairs with him. He smoked at the back door and I went to the toilet at the bottom of the garden.

There were lights on at other houses. I wondered what Santa had brought them. Maybe Santa got caught by someone. I wondered if he got to Phillip and Anne's house. Maybe they got something nice. Maybe they got to it and open things like I saw in my books and on the television.

When my mum and dad was ready we got to go to the front room. There were piles by the tree with our names on. My mum put the television on. It was a programme about kids in the hospital. It was bad they got sick at Christmas. I watched as they took presents to the kids there. They sat at the hospital beds and made them happy, even though they were sick. I wished I could have them at my house. Then they didn't have to be at hospital on Christmas day. I would be sad if I had to be there.

I didn't open anything until my mum said I could. I didn't get a lot. My brother had lots and lots of big boxes. He got Lego and cars and guns and army people. When my mum said I could open mine I didn't want to yet. I wanted it to be a surprise. But she told me to. I got some books, a jigsaw and some clothes.

My brother got a special present. They hid it behind the chair for him. It was big and heavy. My dad lifted it over and put it down. My brother opened it. It was a bike for him. It got three wheels on it. My mum told my brother to sit on it to see if it fit. It did. He liked it a lot.

When it was all done. I got my books and got Mr. Ted and we sat by the fire in the back room. My mum and dad had to start cooking. My brother got his toys to play with. My brother asked me if I could make his Lego. I got good at making Lego. But I felt sad making his. I wished I got some. I liked to play with it. But my mum said my Lego had to be his now.

I asked my brother if I could play when I made it. He said yes. I sat on the floor and pulled out the papers. It got pictures to make it. I did it and counted the bricks. My brother couldn't count yet. I could. I could count really long too. Sometimes I did that at night time when I wanted to stay awake. I didn't like to think about the bad man in case it made him come. Counting made my badness in my brain stay away.

My dad made us all bacon and eggs. He said we could drink tea too. I got my own mug of it. When the food was all gone. My mum started to make the Christmas dinner and my dad was going to get my Nan. I asked if I could go too. He said yes.

We drived to my Nans house. It didn't be far away. But she had presents. She said Santa left some at her house too. I didn't want to wait to get home. But my Nan said I had to. When we got home my Nan sat on the big chair and she gave us the presents. I got chocolate and a garage. It was like a case. It opened up. It had three big ramps on it. There was a bell at the end and I got two cars with it. I told my Nan thank you.

I got to play all day. When dinner got ready my mum told me to make the table. She didn't talk to me all day. I didn't get my medicine. I tried not to make her mad. I had heard her shouting at my Nan in the kitchen. She told my Nan that she smelled bad and said that she always got in the way. She told her to keep out. She said my Nan was a nosey old bat. I didn't think so. My Nan was nice.

It was dark time when my Nan got to go home. My dad said I had to help my mum. He said I could make the dishes dry while she cleaned them. He took my Nan home.

My mum got to be tired. She said she didn't sit down and was tired. My dad said that he would take us to bed. We put all our toys away. My dad said he would read us both a story.

My brother got to sleep before my dad got to read a lot. Maybe he was tired from all his playing. I didn't want to sleep. I didn't want it to not be Christmas day. I liked how Christmas felt inside. It made me feel nice and warm. I wished it could be like that forever.

My brother snored in his sleep. My dad hugged up to me. He put his hand on me and pulled my pyjama bottoms down. He didn't take them off. My tummy got funny inside. It did when my dad hugged me at bed time. My dad took his own pants off and he squashed me against him.

He hugged his face to mine and he kissed me next to my ear. He read the book to me. His mouth made my ear warm. My dad put his finger in his mouth and then he put his hand to my bottom. He tried to do what the bad man did with his thing. But my dad used his finger. I wiggled away. I didn't want my dad to hurt me like the bad man did.

My dad hugged me more. I could feel his thing. He told me that I was a good boy. He used his finger on my bottom and pushed it inside. I didn't like it. It hurt and made me cry. My dad told me I was being really good. He said I was great.

Mr Ted.

Why do I have to do those things? My brother doesn't. Why don't they like me? Why does my brother get to be good and I just be bad and then my daddy does them things.

# DEAR TEDDY

## TWENTY SEVEN

Little boy, little boy,
Pretend to be asleep,
Close your eyes hold my paw,
Your secrets, I'll keep.

My dad fell to sleep when he finished the reading. I didn't know why. Maybe it was my badness. I couldn't get my eyes to stop. They wanted to cry. My dad didn't hurt me. Not like the bad man did. I felt funny inside. It made me hug in a ball. I hugged Mr. Ted and went to sleep. The bad man didn't get to come because my dad was there.

When it got to light time my dad woke me up. He asked me if I wanted to come and get breakfast. I did. I had got to eat Christmas dinner. It was lots and lots. I thought I would pop.

My dad let me use the bathroom in the house. He waited for me outside the door. Then we went down the stairs. He got himself a mug of tea and he asked me if I wanted some too. I did. I asked my dad if

I could have sugar and he said yes. My dad got to the door and he smoked a cigarette like he did every morning. I didn't know why my dad got me up.

He let me put on the television. They got Christmas cartoons on there. I had not watched them before. My dad was in the kitchen. He was cooking. I could smell bacon. He made everyone a bacon sandwich. He gave me one and then took one up to my mum in bed. I told him thank you.

I didn't want my mum or dad to get mad at me. So I ate all my sandwich and then I put my plate in the kitchen. I knew we didn't be allowed to wash the plates. I made sure that I put the plate where my mum liked them. She got mad if it was wrong. I told Mr. Ted. We had a list of rules. There was lots and lots of them. We wrote them in our book to be good. I didn't like getting my mum upset. It made the bad man come.

My dad came into the back room again. He said that if I could be good I could play with my new garage. I had to keep it out of the way and not make a mess. "Make sure you clean up after yourself," he said. "You know how hard your mother works."

I did. I promised. I told him that me and Mr. Ted wouldn't make a mess. We put the garage under the dinner table so we be out of the way. I didn't get a lot of cars. I had five. But I liked them and they went fast down the ramp. There was a bell at the end. I tried not to make it a lot of noise. I didn't want my mum to come downstairs and shout because I got too noisy.

I liked the Boxing Day. It felt like Christmas day too. When my brother got up he got to play with me. We made Lego and cars and put it all together. We had lots of laughs. Mr. Ted sat with us and watched. Our mum gave us dinner. She even let us eat it on the floor when we played. She had put a sheet on the table. We got to play with our Lego and car city in a den. We liked it in there. We couldn't go outside because of the sharks and crocodiles. It was only good when we standed on the lines on the floor. When it got dark time my mum said if we played quiet we could still play. She wanted to watch her programs.

My dad got us torches. We got the Christmas chocolate and we ate it in our den. We played quiet. My dad got his beer from the can and he sat and read his book. My Mum watched the television and we got to play. I liked Boxing Day. It was my favourite.

When my mum's program was finished she said we could watch the film that was on television. It got to be star wars films. I didn't like them so much. But I got to sit with my brother. He watched it and I read my book with Mr. Ted. We got to tidy up first though. We made sure it was right. I asked my mum if it was okay. She said yes it was.

My dad said I could have some of his drink. Not his beer in the can. I didn't like that. He made wine in the attic. It was red and strong. I drinked it before. He said because it was still Christmas time I could have some. I said yes. He got me a glass.

It tasted funny. It made my face scrunch up. But not like the lemons. My dad thought it was funny. He laughed. My brother got a sip. He didn't like it. But I did so I drinked it all and my dad said I could have one more glass. That was it. My mum said he shouldn't give us too much wine. He told her it was Christmas and not all the time.

My brother got to be sleepy next to me. I didn't be tired, but my eyes were sleepy. I wanted to read, but my eyes didn't want to let me. The film wasn't finished. My dad said maybe we should go to bed. It was past bed time anyway. He asked if we wanted a story. My brother said yes.

My mum said she would make the place tidy. She had some pots to wash still. She wanted to stay downstairs. Me and my brother we went upstairs and got our pyjamas on. We brushed our teeth and used the toilet. I liked doing that with my brother. It didn't be scary. Our dad was in the bedroom. He had some of his wine with him and a book to read to us.

My brother got in the middle. We all lied down and our dad started reading. My eyes were very sleepy. They closed and went to sleep right away. Even Mr. Ted was sleepy.

When I waked up I had got moved in the bed. My brother was lied across the pillows. I was lied in the middle of the bed. I was on my tummy. I didn't get any pants on. My dad wasn't reading. He leaned on top of me. He didn't have any pants on too. He kneeled between my legs. He pushed his thing against my bottom. I didn't want him to. The bad man did that. It hurt. He put his fingers inside. It made me feel bad in my tummy.

I didn't like my dad to know I was awake. I was shy because it made me feel funny. I pretended to just wake up. I rubbed my eyes and made my mouth yawn. I asked my dad if I could go to the toilet. I did a pretend sleepy voice like I did with Mr. Ted when we played pretend. My dad said I could.

When I got from the toilet my dad had carried my brother to his bed. He didn't look at me. And he didn't say night-night. He told me to go and get into bed. Then he went downstairs. I didn't stop my eyes crying. I hugged Mr. Ted. We had been bad. My dad was mad. I didn't want the bad man to come.

Mr Ted.

## DEAR TEDDY

Please tell my daddy I'm sorry. I'm scared in my tummy. I don't want him to do what the bad man did. It hurts too bad.

## TWENTY EIGHT

Little boy, little boy,
Your Dad is mad,
Just do what he wants,
No need to be sad.

I wished it still got to be Boxing Day. The day after Boxing Day made me feel sad inside. My heart felt like it was sad and being squashed. I didn't be bad on purpose. It was on accident. My badness was just there. All day long. I couldn't get it to leave me alone.

My dad waked me up in the morning. He told me not to wake my mum. I didn't. I got my clothes off the box. I got changed. My dad watched me when I did it. I didn't like him to watch me. It made me feel funny inside my tummy.

My dad told me I had to get my things away. He said I left them out in the back room. I didn't remember leaving them out. He said it was a right mess and I better get it cleaned up before my mum saw it. When I got downstairs my things was out all over the floor. I didn't leave them that way. I think my brother did it. He was awake before me. He got to sit in my place by the fire and was watching television. He was watching cartoons. He watched Yogi Bear. I liked Yogi Bear. He made me laugh. He always did silly things and made the Ranger man mad at him. But the ranger didn't shout at Yogi.

My dad caught me watching the television. I didn't sit down. But my eyes keeped looking at it. He told me that I wasn't there to be watching the television and I should get everything cleaned away. He said only when I got to be good did I watch the television. But my brother was watching it so I should stop trying to take it off him. I didn't try. I just keeped looking at it. It was hard to look away.

I made it tidy like my dad said. I got my garage away and my cars. I didn't know if I was allowed to watch television now. I standed very still. Like a rock. I was good at standing still games. My brother had my place. I didn't get to use it. It would be badness to tell him to move.

My dad sat at the table. He got his big giant mug with tea in it. He had the paper. I didn't think he liked it a lot because he didn't read it. Maybe it was boring. I thought the paper was boring. It had no fun things in. Sometimes I got to draw in my Nan's paper. Sometimes my Nan also got comics in her paper. She saved them for me and I got to read them. My mum didn't know. She would get mad because my brother didn't get the comics. But he didn't like to read. He was little.

My Nan was going to take me out. I wanted to ask my dad about it. I think he could read my mind because he said, "Your Nan phoned. I told her you had too much to do today and so couldn't go to town with her."

It felt like my eyes wanted to cry. I didn't let them. I held my breath for a long time so they didn't come. My dad smiled at me. But I didn't want to ask him if I could. I didn't want him to get mad.

My dad asked me what I was going to do that day. I told him I didn't know. I had thought I was going to go out with my Nan. Maybe I could go and see Phillip and Anne. He said if I was going to stay in the house all day I could help my mum. He said I didn't get to be lazy and do nothing. "We all have to pull our weight around the house when we live in a family," he said.

I didn't be brave. I whispered to him if maybe I could play out. He said I could if I thought the back room was tidy enough. I looked around. It was. He said it was ok. He told me to go and get out of his sight.

My mum got out of bed. She came downstairs. She had got a lie-in because she was tired. I fastened my shoe laces. I got to do them all by myself. My Nan showed me. She put a string on a chair arm and I did it with her. I didn't get them as good. But it made me do my own shoes. My Nan said I did it very good. She said I was the fastest learner she ever saw.

My mum asked why I was getting my shoes on. My dad told her I was going out to play. But I didn't get my cure yet, she said. She got mad.

"Kitchen," he shouted at me. I wanted to get invisible. I didn't get any breakfast. I didn't like getting my medicine with no breakfast. It made my tummy hurt from the sick inside. But no food got to come out. Stupid boy. I knew I didn't get my medicine yet. I didn't tell my dad. He would make me wait. I always got to be bad. All the time.

My mum said I had to stand in the kitchen. She said over there. I didn't sit on the stool. I keeped getting in her way. When I standed by the fridge she shouted at me to move. When I standed by the sink she said bad words to me and told me to get out of the way. I didn't know where I was to stand.

She got mad at me. She stood big and tall. I had to look up at her. Like a giant. She was like being at the top of the beanstalk. She was mad. She had hair that was mad too. She didn't put it in her braids. It looked funny. "How can I get on when you are always in the way and under my damn feet?" she asked. I didn't know. I tried not to be.

My dad came in the kitchen. He asked my mum what I had done this time. He got my arms and digged his fingers in. He made me move to the door.

He squeezed hard. Maybe his fingers touched the bones in my arms. "Stand there," he said.

I didn't move. My mum made my medicine and gave it to me. It was hot. It burned my neck inside. I asked my mum for a drink. I didn't be able to say it properly the medicine made me cough and cry. It made my mouth too hot. She said no, I couldn't have one.

I didn't be able to breathe. It made my tummy hurt when I got sick inside. My mum was mad. She had her arms crossed. She put the bin in front of me to get my sick into. I tried. But it didn't want to come out.

My mum said that she didn't want me to be in the house. She said I got to be in the way all the time and I should go out. I didn't feel very good. But I did go out. I went to Phillip and Anne's house. They weren't in. I didn't get to go home. My mum would get mad at me.

I went to the beach. It got to be just at the other way from the house. I had to cross the zebra crossing where the boy got knocked over. But I knew how to cross by myself. My Nan had told me. There didn't be anyone for me to talk to. I sat and made a hole in the sand. But the sea started to come back. I had to go back up to the other side of the chains.

It didn't be time for me to go home yet. I didn't know what to do so I walked along one side until I got to the pier my Nan had taken me to. Then I walked back again. Maybe my Nan was still in town. But I didn't know where she would be. I wished I had been able to go. I liked going out with my Nan.

When it got to six. I got back to the house. I went in the back door because I didn't be allowed to use the front door. I didn't know why. But my dad said I wasn't allowed. When I used it he got mad and he hit me. My mum said I should stop thinking I was so important.

My mum was sat on the floor in front of the fire. She was watching television. My dad was sat on a chair. He was drinking his wine and reading a library book. My brother was sat at the floor playing with his Lego. My mum was helping him. They made a house together.

I had never ever played my toys with my mum. She didn't like to. She said she didn't have the time. And that I didn't play very good.

My mum went into the kitchen when I came into the back room. She started to shout my dad. He swore when he got out of his chair. He went in the kitchen too. Then he shouted my name. He was mad. His voice wasn't nice. He swore and told me to come to the kitchen.

I did. My tummy felt funny inside. It made me need to go to the toilet.

"What is this?" he said. He showed me the floor. I had got sand on it from my shoes. It was on accident. I told my dad I was sorry. The brush was keeped under the sink. My mum standed with her arms folded. She was in the way. I tried to get the brush from behind the curtain. My arm knocked things over and lots fell out of the cupboard.

My mum got mad. She swore and shouted at me. She got my arm and pulled me away. She made me fall over. She was mad because one of the bottles got open. Some of the stuff went on the floor. Now she had lots to clean up. "Do you think all I want to do is spend my day cleaning up the shit after you?" she asked me. I shook my head. I didn't do it big because I didn't want to make my eyes cry.

I told my mum I would clean it up. She said not to bother because I would make more mess. She shouted at me that she didn't want any kids and maybe she should just send me to live somewhere else.

Mr Ted.

I never get it right. Maybe they should send me away and then I won't make them sad. Maybe I should go away.

## TWENTY NINE

Little boy, little boy,
Your brothers on his way,
It isn't his fault,
It's just a game to play.

I liked it when we got to be back at school. I liked the way the school smelled. I got happy when it was time to go back. I was going to do my bestest work. My Nan said if I did good at school she would help me get something for my mum. It got to be her birthday soon. It was in February. Like pancake day. But my mum didn't like pancakes so she didn't eat them for her birthday. I got them at my Nans house instead.

My mum liked music. She had lots of records She liked to listen to them in the light time. My Nan showed me which one to get. It was two pounds. I didn't have any money. But my Nan said if I got to be good she would help me to get it. I got happy in my tummy. When I went in the shop I always checked that no one else got it. My Nan said it was okay. She said it would still be there.

When we got back to school. My brother got to go to play school. He just started it. He liked it lots. I didn't like that he got waked up before me. He liked to waked me up. He sneaked into the bedroom and got my mum's brush and then bashed it in my face. He made my nose bleed. It went all over my clothes. I tried to keep it in my hand but it was too runny and fell onto my pyjamas.

My dad said it was funny. My brother didn't get told off. Because my brother didn't be bad. He was just playing. I asked my brother to get me some toilet paper. I didn't be allowed in there. He asked if he could see my nose first. I didn't want to show him. It made the blood go on the floor. But he wouldn't get the tissue until I showed him.

It made it bad when I got the sick in my tummy from my medicine. My nose was sniffy and I didn't be able to breathe from it. My mum said I should breathe from my mouth. But that made the hot stuff burn my mouth inside. I just got to cry because maybe my head wanted to pop open. It made it hurt inside. My mum told me to not be soft.

My brother waked the next day and then the next day. He keeped bashing my face to waked me up too. I wished my mum and dad would make him stop it. When it got to be Sunday again. I got to go to the church. I had to get up very early so my mum woke me first. They left me to get dressed. I didn't get out of bed yet. My brother came in. He didn't be good at being sneaky. I knew he was going to be there.

I got the little radio from the floor. I hid under the covers like a scary monster. Scary monsters didn't get hit. My brother came in. I tried to keep my laugh inside when he was near me. Then I jumped out at him. He lifted something to bash my face. I got the radio and bashed his face first. He screamed loud. His nose had blood and so did his head.

My dad ran up the stairs. He wanted to see what had happened. He picked my brother up and gave him a hug. He got a towel and made his nose not bleed. He shouted my mum. She came up the stairs too. My dad told my mum that I hit my brother. My mum looked at me. She had mad eyes and face. She picked my brother up and taked him downstairs and left me with my dad. She didn't talk to me.

My dad sat on the bed. He made me stand in front of him. I didn't want to look at his face. I was sorry for making my brother cry.

"Why?" he said. I didn't know. I shrugged at my shoulders and watched my feet.

My dad got my face and made me look. He used his fingers under my chin to make me look. He asked me why again. I told him that I was making my brother jump like a scary monster. Because he did it to me.

My dad said that I was the oldest. "You should know better than he does, he is just three years old. You're supposed to be his big brother. Not a bully. We don't accept bullying here."

I got sad in my tummy. I didn't want to be a mean brother. I didn't want to make him cry. I loved my brother lots and lots. He was the best brother in the world. My dad shouted at me about being bad to people. He told me that if you got bad to people then the police came and they took you to jail.

"Do you want to go to jail?"

I shaked my head.

He said I didn't get to go to the library on the weekend after. He said he had enough of me. He didn't want to take a bad boy out with him. I didn't deserve to get nice things.

When we got downstairs my mum got my medicine. She didn't talk to me. She didn't want to be my friend. The medicine was too hot. It made me cough and cry. When my sick from my tummy was gone my mum told me to stand by the wall. I didn't be allowed to look at anyone. They didn't want to see me.

I wished I had Mr. Ted. I got too bad. The bad man would come. My eyes cried. I was scared about the bad man. I got too bad. He would hurt me bad too. Like before

I got to stand in the corner a long, long time. My brother got sweets because his face hurt. He got to watch the television. I didn't because of my badness. My legs hurt. I was tired. I wanted to lie down and go to sleep. Maybe I did get to sleep. I didn't remember the day. It was dark time when I waked up. I didn't know I had gone to bed.

I shouted my mum. I got scared inside and I hided under the covers. I didn't want to see things. I didn't close my eyes. I didn't like when they were closed. I keeped seeing scary pictures. They made my eyes cry. I tried not to cry loud. I didn't want the bad man to hear me.

My mum came upstairs. She said I just had a bad dream. She didn't let me tell her what it was. She said I should go to sleep again. She didn't stay upstairs. I wished she didn't go downstairs. I looked out from a little hole. I was scared.

The scary pictures didn't go away. I dreamed I got to be at the church. In the room next to the fishes. The bad man was there with Brother Marcus. I got to be lied down. They got to hurt me with something hard. They were getting rid of my evilness. They put it inside like the bad man did with his thing. It hurt inside. They wanted to make my bones break. I cried because it hurt. I tried to make myself away from them. But I didn't get to move and they didn't stop. They just made it hurt more.

The scary pictures had lots of red. There was blood on my tummy. It was from the thing that got rid of my evilness. They keeped putting it there and back again. My brother got to be sat on a chair. He was crying and my mum was holding him so he didn't get away.

I didn't like the bad dreams. It keeped being in my brain. I made myself think of nice things. I tried to think about my Nan and the music for my mum. I hoped she would like it a lot. I tried to think about Mr. Ted. But I keeped seeing the pictures.

Mr Ted.

Please me the bad dreams go away. I don't like them. They don't get to stop.

## THIRTY

Little boy, little boy,
It's her birthday,
She doesn't care,
You're just in her way.

    I didn't get to stop the pictures. They were scary. I didn't like to look at them. They made me want to hide away. When I got to bed. If I got allowed to sleep in the bed. I made myself squashed up in a ball. I got the covers so there didn't be any holes for anyone to get me. I got a hole for my nose and mouth and eyes. I didn't like when it got hot on my face and I didn't be able to breathe.

    I sneaked through the little hole and watched the door. I didn't want the bad man to be able to sneaked up on me. My brain made pictures about the bad man hiding and then jumping up. I got to see his scary yellow eyes at the hole. I made my breathing quiet then he didn't know I would be there and he couldn't do that.

# DEAR TEDDY

I didn't let my eyes go to sleep. When they closed I made them jump open again. I couldn't go to sleep because then I would come out of the covers and the bad man would get me. He couldn't get me anymore. I wished God would take me away so I could be with my Gaga and I didn't get to be scared any more. I didn't like being scared. It made my arms and legs hurt because I didn't get to move them.

Sometimes the bad man came and sneaked in. I didn't know how. He was like magic. He got his fingers at my back. I pretended I didn't be there and I got to fall asleep.

I didn't remember what the bad man did. But when I waked up I got to be at the bottom of the bed. All my legs would be scratched.

My bad dreams gave me a tummy ache. It was going to be my mum's birthday when we waked up in the morning. I got scared to go to bed. I didn't feel very well. The bad dreams made the sick in my tummy want to be there. I didn't tell my mum. I got scared she would be mad at me for it. I sat by the fire and didn't move. I didn't talk to Mr. Ted either. He just sat next to me. He liked it. He was my friend.

He was excited in his tummy about giving my mum her record. My Nan had bought it and we had wrapped it up in pink paper. It said happy birthday and it got balloons on it. Mr. Ted picked it for her. We got a card too. But I didn't put Mr. Ted's name in it. She didn't like him like I did. She said he didn't be real. But he was. It was a secret though. He pretended to not be alive when the grownups was around.

When my mum had got all her stuff done. She sat by the fire. She got to be in front of me so I didn't get to see the television. She picked her hair brush from the hearth and gave it to me. She asked me if I would brush her hair for her. It was long and black. It went all the way down her back. When I took the bobble away and opened all her hair. It got curly. When I brushed it, it was bouncy. Her hair got so long I had to bend to brush it all.

I didn't talk when I brushed. I didn't want her to get mad and send me upstairs.

"I'm going to the doctor's tomorrow," she said to me. "You can come with me."

I didn't have to be at school. It was the break time. I had a week off. I liked the doctor. I told my mum thank you.

"Maybe he will give me a card for my birthday," she said. "Your grandfather said we are going to get married one day. That he and I are meant to be together."

I would like it if she got married to the doctor. He was nice. He liked me and talked to me about things. My mum and dad be married. That meant they lived together. I didn't know if the doctor would live with us too.

I brushed my mum's hair until it was all nice and straight and long. She didn't get any knots in it. "I love you mummy," I said. I brushed my hand all down her long hair. She told me it was time to go to bed.

I got scared in my tummy about bed time. Mr. Ted was excited in his tummy for my mum's birthday. The bad man didn't come. I didn't sleep a long, long time. I waked when it still was dark time. I could see the sunshine when it got up. It made me think about it having its hat on. I stayed lied down and watched it. It made the curtains be orange when it made it light time.

I wished my mum and dad would wake up so I could give her my present. I wanted to give it to her first. She would like it. My Nan said it was a very nice present. My mum liked to listen to music. Maybe she would listen to it lots when she put her record player on.

When it got time to wake up. My dad got me out of bed. My mum got up too. But she didn't come down the stairs. She wanted to make herself look all nice and pretty. She was seeing the doctor. She got to wear nice clothes. She had a skirt that looked like three shirts. It had dots on it. She said it was called a rar rar skirt.

When my mum came in the back room. We all be sat waiting for her. She looked mad. Maybe I had been bad. I got scared she wanted to shout.

My mum sat in the chair and my dad made me and my brother sit on the floor. He made breakfast. He said we had to wait. But I didn't want to. I got to feel it in my tummy. My Nan said that was called butterflies. I didn't want butterflies in my tummy. They were for girls.

When my dad came back. He sat down too. I got to give my mum my present first. She said thank you and made it open. My face had a big smile. I waited for my mum to smile too. But she didn't. She looked mad. With her mad eyes. She stared at me. I got scared she was going to shout at me.

"What did you buy this for?" she said.

I didn't know I had been bad. I made my shoulders shrug up and down.

"Perhaps in the future you shouldn't buy things you don't know anything about. It was a waste of money and we don't have money to waste," she said.

I told my mum that I got to be sorry. She gave me the record and told me to put it in the rubbish bin. My eyes wanted to cry. I didn't let them. I made my breath stay inside and my mouth didn't get to open.

I went in the kitchen. I could hear my mum laugh. My brother laughed too. Maybe he had got her something nice. I made the record break into bits. I put it in the bin. I didn't go in the back room. It made me feel sad. I was sorry I didn't do it right.

I sat at the steps where my mum and dad smoked their cigarettes. I hugged my knees and let my eyes cry on them. I told my mum in my brain that I was sorry for being such a bad boy.

Mr Ted.

I don't know why my Mummy didn't want the present. I thought it got to be good. I get everything wrong.

## THIRTY ONE

Little boy, little boy,
Help your Mum,
Listen to her,
You are her son.

When my mum got her breakfast all finished and she had ate all her breakfast things. She came into the kitchen. I standed on my feet. I didn't want her to shout at me for sitting on the step. Maybe it would get my clothes dirty. She would say that if I was going to sit on the ground she might as well not waste her time making my clothes nice and clean again.

My mum went to the backdoor. She smoked her cigarette. I didn't talk to her. I didn't know if she wanted me to. Maybe she was still mad at me. I didn't want to ask in case she shouted at me again. I didn't know to say about my medicine. I had not got it yet. Maybe she forgot. My dad said when people forgot lots of things it was because they had the brains of a hen. He said I had the brains of a hen all the time. He said the only reason I got to have nice things was because I got to be such a nice looking boy. He said when people looked like me. I didn't need the brains. I just tricked it from people.

I didn't know what kind of boy my dad meant. My dad said I was that kind of boy. He said it one day I was in the bath and he got his hand on my thing. I didn't want to be that kind of boy. I didn't want people to touch me like that. It hurt. But my dad said it's how to get nice things. If I got to be nice back.

My mum finished her cigarette and we was going to walk to the doctor's. She didn't want my dad to take her. When he asked she shouted at him. She said he had to look after my brother. It didn't get to be far to the doctors.

We walked. My mum didn't walk as fast as me. She keeped stopping and talking to people. They always talked about boring things. I got to stand next to her and be quiet. Lots of people said happy birthday to her. They asked me if I had got my mum anything nice. I didn't say anything. I smiled. I didn't want them to know I got my mum a bad present and made her sad. They would do that bad face that made me feel more sad inside.

When we got nearly there. My mum stopped. She keeped looking behind us. She looked scared in her face. I asked her if she was okay. She said she didn't feel very well. I knew my mum didn't like to feel sick outside. It made her scared. It made her think someone bad would come.

I told my mum we was nearly at the doctors. I said he liked her very much and it was her birthday. I told her she should think about the doctor and it would make it better. That is what I did when I was scared. I made my brain think of different pictures that I liked.

My mum asked me if the doctor would be happy to see her. I said he would. She got to be the birthday girl today. He was always nice to her.

After we had sat in the waiting room forever and ever. The lady from the office at the front. The mean looking one. Another nosey old bag my mum said. Even my Nan said she was a nosey old bag. So maybe she really was. Maybe she was a big one because lots of people said it. The lady said it was my mum's turn to see the doctor.

I didn't get to go inside with her. It made me sad because he told me about being a doctor and I got to look at all the pictures on his wall. But my mum said that I didn't get to go because it was her birthday and maybe he would give her a kiss. I didn't be scared to wait by myself. I sat on the chair my mum had used. There were lots of comics to read. They were old and I had read lots of them already. But I read them again. They were still fun.

When my mum came to get me after she had seen the doctor. She looked like she was happy. She had a big bright smile on her face. Like the smiles I got when I got to be excited.

I asked my mum if she got a card. She said no. She said that she knew it was because he was married. She said when people are married like that; they couldn't buy other ladies birthday cards. "The doctor's wife is horrible," she said. "If he was to buy me a card his wife would make him lose his job and then he wouldn't be able to be a doctor anymore. She is selfish and just wants him for his money. She doesn't love him like I do. She would make him sad."

I thought she must be a nasty lady. Like the bullies at school. It didn't be fair to be mean to the doctor. He was a nice man. He was always nice to me and other people. He spended all his time making people better. He was nice. She shouldn't be bad to him like that.

My mum said the mean wife had an ugly face. I said maybe she looked like a horse. That is what it said in one of my books. Me and Mr. Ted had laughed. The bullies had said the girl had a horse face. But she didn't. She was pretty. But not like the doctors wife. She was mean and ugly.

My mum said I was right. She said maybe the wife did look like a horse. I told her maybe the wife had big teeth like a horse. And a big giant nose. My mum agreed.

When we walked out of the doctors. We got into the bit where all the cars got parked. She showed me the doctor's car. It was big and black. It looked like a racing car I had in my garage at home. Maybe it got to be very fast too. Like the bat mobile. I told my mum maybe he had a car like batman. "Maybe he drives like batman too," she said. My mum said that we could call him batman. Then it got to be a secret. She said it had to be a secret because if his wife got to know the secret then she would be mean.

We talked all the way home about batman. Dr Batman not the real one. I didn't think my mum would like real batman. When we got home my mum said I could go and play out with my friends. She said I could call for Phillip and Anne. But I got to be back early because it was her birthday and we had an early dinner. It would be a birthday dinner. I wondered if she was going to have some cake. Maybe she would get candles on it too. I had never got a birthday cake before. And I didn't get candles.

I played with Phillip and Anne all day long. We got some skates. Anne let me use some of hers. They were too big for me. But I liked them. They were blue and had red lines on them. They had a big yellow stopper at the front so I didn't get rolled away on them. I didn't know how to skate. It was scary. My feet got run away. I held the wall all along. I walked on the skates. Anne wanted to show me how to do it properly. She got to go very fast. I wished I could do that. I didn't want to fall over.

We went around the block. Anne told me to let go of the wall. She holded my hand and skated at the side of me. She pulled me. I squeezed her hand with mine. Phillip didn't be able to skate. He stayed by the wall. Anne said it was because he was a scardey cat.

I didn't be a scardey cat.

When it was time to go home. I gave Anne her skates. In the house they had all the birthday things ready. My mum said that she had some news to tell me and my brother. She told us that she was going to have a new baby. She said that there was a new baby in her tummy and maybe we would get a new brother.

Mr Ted,

Maybe if my Mummy got married to the doctor, she would get to be happy?

## THIRTY TWO

Little boy, little boy,
He's your Dad,
He's going to hurt you,
He'll make you sad.

I didn't want a new brother. I didn't want to get a sister. My mum and dad didn't like me. I didn't be good. They wouldn't love me any more if there was a new baby. New babies always got to be nice. My mum's friend had a new baby and then she didn't spend time with the girl. If my mum got a new baby she would hate me. Because I didn't be a cute baby. I was evil. She didn't want me.

I didn't play with my brother. My mum didn't want me to give him my evilness. I didn't be able to touch the new baby. I didn't want to give it my evilness too. The baby wouldn't have evilness and they would like it better than me. I told my mum I didn't want a new brother or sister. My mum said it didn't matter. I was going to get one. I crossed my arms over and I shouted at her. I told her I didn't want a new brother or sister.

She shouted back at me. "You spoil everything," she said. "This is my good news and you're spoiling it. Get upstairs." I shaked my head. I shaked it hard to see I was mad like she got. I said no and squeezed my mouth closed tight.

My dad got my arm. He dragged me out of the backroom and pushed me into the hallway. He told me to get up the stairs now and to the bedroom. I wanted to shout at him too. My eyes wanted to cry. He yelled at me to get up those stairs. "Or else."

I got bad. My foot kicked on the side of the stair. I made a growl noise like a monster because my badness was inside. It wanted to come out and make me do lots of bad things. I banged my feet on the stairs when I went up them. When I got to the top. I could see my bedroom. I got scared in my tummy. Maybe the bad man would come because I was being bad.

My dad was still waiting. He shouted at me to go to the bedroom and sit on the box. He told me not to make any noise or I would get in bigger trouble. I did get upstairs and I did sit on the box. I hugged my legs. I didn't be able to stop the crying.

I didn't want a brother. Maybe God would make it not real. If I got a brother my mum would love it more. Like she did with my brother. She liked him more than me. He was her friend. I just be bad all the time. If they got a new baby maybe I would get sent away. My mum didn't want me. She might send me to the children's house. They put children there that didn't be wanted anymore.

I heard my dad's feet coming up the stairs. I dried my face. I didn't want him to know that I got to cry. He would call me a baby. He always said I was a baby when I cried. I didn't like being a baby.

He came in the bedroom. He closed the door. I wondered if he was mad. He didn't look mad. Not like when he got to shout at me. He sat in the bed. I looked at my feet. I wished I had Mr. Ted. But he was still in the bed. I had forgot to pick him up. I didn't want to look at my dad's face. I didn't want to see if he got mad at me.

My dad said that a new baby wasn't a bad thing. "It isn't the end of the world, you know," he said. "Lots of families got new babies. It doesn't mean that something bad will happen. Besides, you get to be a big brother."

I already did be a big brother. I didn't want to be a big brother again. They would like the baby more than me because I was so bad all the time. I got to be evil inside. I didn't want to make the new baby evil. I didn't be allowed near my brother in case he got the evil.

My dad said that mums and dads could love lots of children. Maybe one or one hundred. I didn't want one hundred babies in the house. It be my job to be the big brother to love them and hug them and make sure no one hurt them. Maybe I needed my big brother. But he lived in a different house with a new mum and dad and he got to be sad all the time because he missed his real mum and dad.

My dad came and sat next to me on the box. He got big and heavy. I wondered if it might break into a million pieces. My dad said that when the baby came my mum would get very tired and then she would need lots of help. I got to be a big special brother because I was the biggest and got to go to school and lots of things like that. It made me more special.

My dad put me on his knee. I had not got to be on his knee before. He let my brother sit on his knee sometimes, but not me. I got to be bad all the time and spoiled everything so he didn't like it. Maybe now I got to be a big special brother I could not be as evil inside. My dad gave me a hug. I gave him a hug too. He smelled like his beer and cigarettes and his motorbike.

My dad lifted me off his knee. It was super fast like Superman with special powers. I nearly got to fly and land on the bed in front of us. I landed on my tummy. My dad opened my pants. He took them off. He took my underpants off too. He opened his own pants too. I tried to get off the bed. But my dad squashed me down. He was big and strong. I was just little. I didn't get to grow yet. He did what the bad man did. I didn't know he was going to do it. I didn't know I was in trouble for being bad. I thought my dad was being nice to me. He got his thing and he pushed it inside. Like the bad man.

It hurt very bad. It made me cry. I didn't be able to stop the cries because my dad's thing hurt me. It made my tummy want to get sick and my head wanted to explode. I cried really loud. I didn't get able to say any words to make my dad stop. My dad put his hand on my mouth. He squeezed it closed. But I still had to cry. My nose all filled up and I didn't be able to breathe. My dad didn't get to stop. I was sorry for shouting at my mum. I was sorry for everything.

My dad let go. He got off me and stopped squashing me down. He got my clothes off the floor and put them on the bed. He got his own pants back up. I didn't get up. I stayed lied on the bed. I didn't move my legs because it hurt inside. I got cold. But I didn't move. My dad said he was going to make me a bath. He left the bedroom.

I didn't get to stop it. I cried on the bed. I tried to make my legs move so I could hug them. I didn't be able to because my dad had hurt me. It made me cry lots more when I tried. It made my breath go away and my head want to go to sleep.

My dad came back. He said my bath was ready and I should get in it before I got to go back down stairs. He told me to go to the bathroom. Maybe my dad would be mad with me because I didn't be able to walk properly. It hurt to make my legs move. I didn't be able to get my pants on. I got blood on my legs. My dad got my clothes and cleaned it away. I didn't walk very fast. I tried not to cry loud. I didn't want to make my mum mad with my noise.

I didn't be able to get in the bath. My legs hurt too much. When I tried to climb over it made me hurt inside and made me cry. My dad lifted me up. The water didn't be too deep and it was cold. I didn't tell him. Maybe it would be bad and he would do the thing to me again. I didn't want to make him mad. I sat still. Like a statue.

My dad cleaned me all up. He put my pyjamas on and told me to go down stairs. I got to put underpants with my pyjamas. My mum always said I didn't do that. But my dad said I had to. My dad told me to go downstairs and not make my mum upset again. I didn't. I didn't be bad to anyone. I lied by the fire and hugged my tummy. I closed my eyes. I didn't be bad ever again.

Mr Ted.

Please tell my daddy I'm sorry. I'm sorry for being a bad boy. I didn't mean to shout at them about the new baby. I don't want a new baby. It will make them send me away.

Contact

dearmrted@gmail.com

http://jdstockholm.com/

http://www.facebook.com/dearmrted

These two sites have been invaluable to me throughout the last few years. I salute the many people on there, survivors, directors and above all, my friends. Thank you for the support at those times I needed it.

http://www.isurvive.org.uk

http://www.recoveryourlife.com/

Printed in Great Britain
by Amazon